**Carolyn Humphries** has been a food writer and editor for many years. She started her career as a chef, but quickly realised she preferred to create food for people to cook at home. Having trained as a journalist, she became a food writer for *Woman* magazine. She has since written for numerous magazines, is the author of more than 60 books and has been a consultant, co-writer and editor on many more projects. She is a member both of The Guild of Food Writers and the Institute of Health Promotion and Education.

*Other titles*

Everyday Family Recipes for Your Combination Microwave

Everyday Lebanese Cooking

A Lebanese Feast

Patisserie

How To Make Your Own Cordials and Syrups

Southern Italian Family Cooking

How To Make Perfect Panini

Afternoon Tea

Everyday Thai Cooking

Everyday Curries

The Healthy Slow Cooker Cookbook

Everyday Bread from Your Bread Machine

# THE SPIRALIZER COOKBOOK

Carolyn Humphries

**A How To Book**

ROBINSON

ROBINSON

First published in Great Britain in 2016 by Robinson



1 3 5 7 9 10 8 6 4 2



A CIP catalogue record for this book
is available from the British Library.

ISBN: 978-1-47213-739-5 (paperback)

Typeset in by Basement Press, Glaisdale
Printed and bound in Great Britain by Clays Ltd, St Ives plc

Papers used by Robinson are from well-managed forests and other responsible sources.

Robinson
is an imprint of
Little, Brown Book Group
Carmelite House
50 Victoria Embankment
London EC4Y 0DZ

An Hachette UK Company
www.hachette.co.uk

www.littlebrown.co.uk

How To Books are published by Robinson, an imprint of Little, Brown Book Group. We welcome proposals from authors who have first-hand experience of their subjects. Please set out the aims of your book, its target market and its suggested contents in an email to Nikki.Read@howtobooks.co.uk.

# CONTENTS

# INTRODUCTION

Noodles are a favourite staple in many parts of the world. But with an increasing number of people wanting to reduce the amount of processed white flour they consume (and not keen on wholewheat varieties) and so many others on low-carb or weight-reducing diets, vegetable noodles made with a spiralizer are becoming very popular as brilliant alternatives to pasta. Vegetable ribbons aren't new but they were always rather laborious to create with a potato peeler and resulted in wide thin strips rather than spaghetti-like threads. Plus they could only be as long as the vegetable you were shaving. A spiralizer enables you to make myriad colourful, fresh-tasting noodles in varying thicknesses. You can chop them to make 'rice' or other grain alternatives or use in place of coarsely grated vegetables, too.

We are all encouraged to eat a rainbow of vegetables and fruit every day as different colours have different health-promoting properties. If we include a good range in our diet, we'll get the maximum benefit, as they are packed with vital vitamins, minerals for our general well-being, and loads of phytonutrients (which are thought to help protect us against some cancers and heart disease, can help reduce blood-cholesterol levels, osteoporosis and boost our immune systems). They also supply soluble and insoluble fibre that aids digestion and helps keep us fit and healthy. But lots of people find it hard to plough through a plateful of veggies or chomp their way through whole pieces of fruit. But when spiralized, they become a fun way to get more of your (minimum) five-a-day as they not only look appetising, they slip down so easily!

Eating a low-carb diet every day is not something I endorse, unless it is for medical reasons, because high-fibre, starchy carbohydrates – such as wholemeal and rye breads, oats, barley, millet, brown rice, wholemeal or buckwheat pasta, pulses, potatoes, sweet potatoes and yams – are an essential part of a balanced diet to give you slow-release energy, masses of nutrients and to help keep your digestion working properly. But there is no denying that a low-carb diet can help you lose weight. Also, if you are diabetic and need to keep your blood sugar levels constant, you will need to watch your carbs, too – particularly the processed white ones that can cause your blood sugar levels to fluctuate in the same way that sugary foods do – and these gorgeous alternatives to white pasta and rice are a delicious boon.

Because this book isn't solely for people on low-carb diets, I have often given starchy carb suggestions as extra additions to the recipes or as serving suggestions. Do have them unless you really need to be on a low-carb diet as they will ensure that you have all the nutrients you need for balanced meals and the bulk to keep you sustained for several hours.

Whatever your motives for wanting to give spiralizing a go, this book is packed with great ideas for breakfasts through starters and light meals, main courses, snacks, side dishes, desserts and some great bakes (as spiralizing is so much quicker and easier than grating veggies to add to breads and cakes). So give your fruit and vegetables a twirl and create tasty, fun meals packed with goodness that all the family will enjoy.

## NOTES ON THE RECIPES

- In most cases the recipes are designed for four people but this depends on appetites and some may feed fewer hungry adults! If you want a different number of servings, most recipes can easily be doubled, quartered or halved accordingly.
- The ingredients are listed in the order in which they are used in the recipe.
- When I call for a knob of butter it should be about 15g, and a large or good knob is about 30g, but the exact amount is not crucial to the recipe, so it's easier just to cut off a bit you gauge to be about the right size rather than bothering to weigh it!
- A handful is the amount of the ingredient you can comfortably hold in the palm of your hand. As with a knob of butter, the quantity is not vital, so use your own judgement.
- All spoon measures are level unless otherwise stated. 1 tsp = 5ml, 1 tbsp = 15ml.
- Eggs and vegetables are average, medium-sized unless otherwise stated.
- All can and packet sizes are approximate as they vary from brand to brand.
- In some recipes I have told you to cut noodles into specific lengths (or chop for 'grains'), but in others, where long strands are desirable, I have not said to cut them. However, you may find that some strands are too long to eat easily in spaghetti-style recipes, so use your initiative and cut into manageable lengths, if you prefer.
- Seasoning is very much a matter of personal taste. Taste the food as you cook and adjust to suit your own palate.
- Cooking times are approximate and should be used as a guide only. Always check food is piping hot and cooked through before serving.
- Always preheat the oven and cook on the shelf just above the centre unless otherwise stated (this isn't necessary in a fan oven where the heat is similar throughout the oven).

# CHAPTER 1
# CHOOSING AND USING A SPIRALIZER

There are three main types of spiralizer: side-winding machines, top-winding machines and little hand-held models. This book is designed for use with larger top-winders or side-winders, but many of the recipes would work if you only have a hand-held gadget.

I have a top-winding model, which was recommended highly. It can tackle even fairly small foods and only leaves a tiny piece unspiralized at the end. The downside is that all the curls or noodles collect underneath the machine. This can sometimes clog it, so you have to stop and remove them before continuing with the remaining vegetables. The plus is the machine is very stable on the worktop, which is helpful as you are pressing downward all the time.

Side-winders collect all the food in front of the machine so you can make a large amount without having to stop and clear them. I gather they do tend to leave quite a big piece of food at the end of spiralizing and don't tackle smaller items as well (but that is just hearsay).

The hand-held spiralizers are self-explanatory and are more like using a potato peeler in as much as they take rather more time and effort. If you haven't bought one already, I think there is little to choose between the larger models; just make sure the one you choose can be secured firmly to the work surface and is a model that is easy to clean (mine is all plastic except for the blades themselves and can easily be washed or wiped down). Always wash in hot soapy water and rinse well. Many spiralizers are dishwasher proof. Check your manufacturer's instructions.

Please take care when using your spiralizer as the blades are razor sharp and the holder spikes are like needles, too. I have several scars to remind me how careful you need to be when putting a blade in place, removing it, fitting or adjusting food on the holder and when washing up.

## TOP TIPS FOR USING YOUR SPIRALIZER

The most annoying thing I discovered when I bought my spiralizer was that there were very few instructions with the machine about what to do, how to do it and how to use the strands once you had made them. So I've been through a lot of trial and error to get to the point of creating 100 recipes that I'm really pleased with and can share with you!

Here are all the little tricks I've learnt along the way on how get the most out of your spiralizer.

- **Use firm fruit and veg:** Always choose very firm, fresh fruit and vegetables. For instance, an aubergine that is even slightly soft will not spiralize. Also a banana or papaya must be completely green – if it has just a hint of a tint of yellowing hue it will be too soft.
- **Avoid soft produce:** Soft fruits and vegetables or any with a soft centre or hole where seeds have been removed, such as pumpkin, will not spiralize. The only exception is very firm peppers as long as you leave them whole with the seeds in place (see note page 8).
- **Scrub:** Scrub or wash and peel produce if necessary.
- **Trim:** Always trim vegetables so they have a flat surface to press the handle into, otherwise the vegetable will not be held securely. Harder vegetables, such as celeriac, need to be flat at both ends whereas fruit, including peppers, are fine as they are (though a very pointed pear may need trimming so it fits easily on the spike).
- **Cut to size:** Halve or cut into pieces if the item is too big to fit between the winder and the blade. For large fat round solid

vegetables, like swede or celeriac, I find it is sometimes easier to cut them in halves or quarters to spiralize them, but it's always best to try them whole first. If the veg won't turn, then remove it and cut it into more manageable pieces, remembering to ensure the pieces have a flat top where they fix to the winder or they won't be held securely.

- **Keep an even pressure:** Always keep an even pressure when turning the handle – too light and the food may well stop cutting after a few turns, too firm and you can squash the item so it breaks or prevent the food turning properly on the blade. You'll soon discover what works right for each item depending on its density.
- **Turn slowly:** Turn slowly and consistently. For some foods, if you turn too quickly, you will end up with short little curls rather than long strands. Again, practice makes perfect!
- **Put the calyx at the end:** For fruit or vegetables with a stump or calyx, place this end towards the handle as this will be the last little bit of the fruit or veg that is discarded at the end of spiralizing.
- **Don't waste the last pieces:** You will always be left with a small piece of fruit or vegetable that can't be spiralized – such as pieces of potato, courgette or carrot. Don't throw these pieces away if you can use them. You may be able to chop them and add them to the dish or set them aside to use in soup or for stock.
- **Use the wide curls blade for veg with layers:** When spiralizing layered veg – such as leeks, onions or cabbage – you must use the wide curls blade, and you'll find loose outer layers peel off on the outside of the spiralizer as you turn. Simply remove them and add to a stock pot or soup, or shred and add to the dish you are making, if appropriate.
- **Cabbage:** When spiralizing cabbage, you may not want thin slices of stump in your finished dish so simply pick them out of your pile of shreds before use and add to stock.

- **Peppers:** When spiralizing peppers you will have quite a few seeds and the core sliced as well, so always pick those out, then rinse the peppers to remove the last of the seeds. There will be a ring of unspiralized pepper round the stalk end. You can slice or chop this to add to your dish, too.
- **Coping with dislodged veg:** Sometimes your vegetable or fruit will dislodge halfway through spiralizing. This usually happens if you don't put quite the right amount of pressure as you turn the handle, the top of the vegetable was not level so the holder didn't grip tightly enough, or, if you have an upright model, because too many noodles have built up underneath and there is no more room for them to freely leave the machine. Just stop, remove the already spiralized noodles, take off the vegetable or fruit, turn it over and start again or, if the tip where the holder has pierced it has damaged the surface, slice off a thin layer and reattach the vegetable or fruit to the holding spike.
- **When veg get stuck:** If the vegetable gets stuck halfway through and won't turn (it sometimes happens, particularly with the really firm ones like parsnip or celeriac) try turning the handle backwards for a couple of turns, then turn it normally again. This usually works but, if not, you will have to take it off the spike, remove any noodles stuck in the blade and re-set it.
- **Take great care with sharp blades:** If your veg stops turning and it seems the holder won't hold it but it is secure on the spike, I don't recommend pulling up the handle and turning the vegetable manually (although it works). I did and sliced my thumb so badly I had to go to hospital, so be warned!

# CHAPTER 2
# SPIRALIZING AS PART OF A HEALTHY DIET

Lovely thin strands or curly ribbons of vegetables or fruit are a fun and appetising way of incorporating more vegetables and fruit into your diet. As everyone acknowledges, if you use them in place of pasta or rice, you can considerably reduce your starchy carbohydrates, which will help you lose weight.

However, for a normal, healthy person, if you just eat non-starchy vegetables and sauce, say, for dinner, you won't have enough 'bulk' to fill you up or give you long-term energy. Many of the dishes in this book do incorporate starchy carbs – any of the potato, sweet potato or yam recipes, for instance – and for others I have included other carbs in the dish. Sometimes I have given suggestions for appropriate foods to serve with the dish, such as wholegrain bread. In other cases – such as Turnip Spaghetti with Tomato and Basil Sauce (see page 114), you could use half the amount of turnip noodles and cook 225g wholewheat spaghetti (or white with added fibre) and mix with the turnip spaghetti before topping with the tomato sauce.

## THE ELEMENTS OF A HEALTHY DIET

A healthy diet should include:

- **Protein:** Essential for growth and repair of all body cells, protein is found in lean meat, fish, poultry, dairy foods, such as cheese and yogurt, pulses (dried peas, beans and lentils), soya products such as tofu, nuts, seeds and avocados. You also get a lot in wholegrains, with amaranth and quinoa topping the list.

- **Carbohydrates:** Giving us energy and warmth, carbs come in two forms. The first, starchy carbs, come from yams, potatoes, sweet potatoes, bread, pasta, rice (preferably wholegrain) and other cereals such as oats, barley and rye and are vital for slow-release energy. Whole grains are better than processed white grains as they contain plenty of nutrients and fibre, essential for a healthy digestion. That doesn't mean you can never enjoy sushi again or a traditional spaghetti bolognese on pearly white strands of egg pasta; it's just worth substituting wholegrain varieties for white most of the time. The second type is simple carbohydrates (sugars) and this is where confusion often arises. It's okay to eat sugar found naturally in fruit, vegetables, nuts, seeds and so on as it is a good source of energy and these foods give you loads of other nutrients and fibre. Refined sugar, on the other hand – the stuff you buy in packets and in syrup form and which is added to foods when they are prepared – just contains 'empty' calories, which can be a cause of obesity and tooth decay. Added sugar should be kept to a minimum and avoided when possible. To sweeten foods in cooking, I prefer to use honey instead, which, although is as calorific as refined sugar and can still cause tooth decay, is thought to have prebiotic properties that encourage the growth of beneficial bacteria in the gut and also contains some vitamins and minerals. It is also sweeter than sugar, so you don't need as much to get the desired flavour.
- **Fruit and vegetables:** These provide fibre for a healthy digestive system, vitamins and minerals for general well-being, and phytonutrients, which contain antioxidants that help protect against some cancers, heart disease and other life-threatening conditions.
- **Dairy produce:** For healthy teeth and bones, include milk, yogurt, cheese and cream in your diet, choosing reduced-fat options if you prefer.

- **Fibre:** For a healthy digestive system and a healthy heart, fibre is found in all plant foods and comes in two forms – both vital. Soluble fibre dissolves in water in our gut and forms a gel. This slows the absorption of glucose into the bloodstream and so stops little surges of sugar when we've just eaten, keeping our energy levels on an even keel. It also helps prevent constipation and helps lower blood cholesterol levels and so helps prevent heart disease. Insoluble fibre is, as it says, insoluble. It's in the fibrous husks of grains, seeds and pulses and the skin and membranes of fruit and vegetables. It passes through our digestive systems, keeping everything soft and moving so we don't get constipated, and helps prevent the build-up of toxins in our bodies.
- **Fats:** Contrary to some people's understanding, some fats are vital for warmth, healthy cells and energy. But you need the right kind of fats and you only need a little. Saturated fats, found in all animal products, are thought to contribute to increased cholesterol levels in the blood, so should be kept to a minimum. Choose lean meat, don't eat the skin on poultry and go for reduced-fat dairy produce if you are at risk. Polyunsaturated and monounsaturated fats, found in plant oils (nuts, seeds, olives, for example) are considered healthier options. However, as part of a normal healthy diet, there is no harm in having a little butter on your bread or using it in cooking for its flavour. Just use it sparingly.
- **Water:** Water is essential for life itself. We need to keep every part of our body hydrated and should drink about eight glasses a day. This can include other liquids but go easy on the caffeine and alcohol and avoid sugary drinks. Pure juices should be drunk as part of a meal as, although they contain only natural sugars, they do coat the teeth in a way that can still cause tooth decay if used as a thirst-quencher during the day. Also, however much pure juice you drink in a day, it only counts as one of your five-a-day as it is more important to eat the entire fruit or vegetable so you get all the nutrients and fibre.

## CHAPTER 3

# COMFORTING BREAKFASTS AND LEISURELY BRUNCHES

For a grab-and-go breakfast, most people don't look for recipes, so I have just included a couple of recipes here that are designed for breakfast in a hurry: Plantain Breakfast Muffins (see page 20), which can be made in advance and are ideal to grab and go, and the Green Banana and Apple Porridge with Cinnamon (see page 13) which, again, can be made beforehand and takes only seconds to put together. The remaining recipes are perfect for weekends, brunches and holidays, when you have time to relax and really enjoy breaking your fast and indulging in a delicious meal at your leisure. Even with these, most of the preparation can be done the night before, if you prefer, so you only have to put the finishing touches to them in the morning.

# GREEN BANANA AND APPLE PORRIDGE WITH CINNAMON

I make this the night before then pop it in the microwave to heat through just before serving. It will keep for several days if you are only serving one person. You can, of course, reheat it in a saucepan by simply stirring it continuously over a medium heat until gently bubbling, adding a splash more milk if necessary. Make sure your bananas are firm and green – soft yellow ones won't do! Also, I find it easiest to peel green bananas with a knife as the outer skin does not come away easily.

**Serves 2–4**

**2 large green bananas, peeled and halved widthways**
**2 eating apples, peeled and stalks removed**
**300ml milk**
**4 tbsp ground almonds**
**2 tsp clear honey, plus extra for drizzling (optional)**
**¼ tsp ground cinnamon**

*To serve*

**extra milk, dried fruit or fresh berries, and some sunflower or pumpkin seeds (all optional)**

1. Spiralize the green bananas on the 5mm noodle blade, then the apples on the same blade, stalk ends towards the blade. Discard any pips. Place in a food processor and pulse briefly to finely chop or chop finely by hand. Tip into a saucepan.
2. Add the remaining ingredients and bring to the boil, then reduce the heat and simmer for about 3 minutes until thick and creamy, stirring occasionally.
3. Either serve immediately with extra milk, honey dried fruit or fresh berries, with some seeds scattered on top, if using, or cool, cover and store in the fridge ready to reheat in the morning.

# APPLE, OAT AND HAZELNUT GRANOLA

This is a delicious, crunchy breakfast cereal. By spiralizing the apple, it becomes so thin that it crisps beautifully when baked with the other ingredients. The cereal is lightly sweetened with honey but is nothing like as sweet as the commercial brands – and a little honey has good prebiotic properties, which means it helps your gut to grow good bacteria to aid your digestion. I've made enough for at least 8 servings, so you can store it in an airtight container to use as required.

**Serves 8–10**

**2 red eating apples, stalks removed**
**225g rolled oats**
**60g hazelnuts, roughly chopped (not too finely)**
**3 tbsp sunflower seeds**
**3 tbsp pumpkin seeds**
**1 tsp ground mixed spice**
**2 tbsp clear honey**
**2 tbsp apple juice or water**

***To serve***
**milk or plain yogurt**

1. Spiralize the apples on the wide curls blade, stalk ends towards the blade. Discard any pips. Snip into roughly 2cm lengths with scissors, a handful at a time.
2. Preheat the oven to 160°C/Gas 3 and line two baking trays with baking paper.
3. Mix the apples with the oats, nuts, seeds and mixed spice in a bowl. Blend the honey and water together and mix in thoroughly.
4. Spread the mixture out on the prepared baking trays. Bake in the oven for 40 minutes until dry and lightly golden, stirring occasionally and swapping the trays over halfway through cooking.
5. Switch off the oven but leave the granola to cool in the oven, then store in an airtight container. Serve with milk or plain yogurt.

# PEAR AND APPLE CURLS WITH VANILLA AND WALNUT YOGURT

I prepare the fruit and put it in a sealed plastic container in the fridge and make up the yogurt separately, then just put the two together at breakfast time. If you are making this to eat straight away, there is no need to toss the fruit in lemon juice.

**Serves 1**

**1 slightly under-ripe pear, stalk end trimmed flat**
**1 eating apple, stalk removed**
**1 tsp lemon juice**
**85g plain yogurt**
**¼ tsp natural vanilla extract**
**15g walnuts, chopped**
**1 tsp clear honey**

1. Spiralize the fruits on the wide curls blade, stalk ends towards the blade. Discard any pips. Toss in the lemon juice until well coated, then put in a sealed container and chill until ready to serve.
2. Mix the yogurt, vanilla, nuts and honey together and chill until required.
3. Pile the fruit curls in a bowl and top with the crunchy nut vanilla yogurt.

# SWEET POTATO PANCAKES WITH MAPLE SYRUP AND BACON

These pancakes can be prepared and cooked the night before, then just reheated briefly in a dry non-stick frying pan for a couple of minutes on either side, or very briefly in the microwave. Alternatively, place them on a covered plate over a pan of gently simmering water or wrap in foil and heat through in a low oven for about 10 minutes.

**Makes 6–8**

**1 fairly small sweet potato, about 225g, scrubbed or peeled and trimmed**
**a large knob of butter**
**115g spelt flour**
**a pinch of salt**
**2 tsp baking powder**
**2 eggs**
**175ml milk**
**groundnut or sunflower oil, for frying**
**6 or 8 smoked back bacon rashers**

***To serve***
**maple syrup**

1. Spiralize the sweet potato on the 3mm noodle blade.
2. Heat the butter in a non-stick frying pan and stir-fry the sweet potatoes over a low heat for about 3 minutes until soft. Tip into a bowl and set aside, then wipe out the pan with kitchen paper.

3 Mix the flour, salt and baking powder together in a bowl. Make a well in the centre and add the eggs and half the milk. Whisk until smooth, then whisk in the remaining milk and stir in the sweet potato ribbons.

4 Heat a little oil in the pan and pour off any excess. Using a large serving spoon, drop a large spoonful of the sweet potato mix into the pan and spread out with the back of the spoon to a pancake about 12–14cm in diameter. Fry over a medium heat for a few minutes until almost set, bubbles appear and burst on the surface and the base is golden brown. Flip the pancake over and brown the other side. Slide onto a plate and keep warm while making the remaining pancakes in the same way.

5 When the pancakes are nearly ready, grill or fry the bacon until browned on both sides. Serve one or two pancakes, according to appetite, with the bacon on top and drizzled with maple syrup.

# POTATO NOODLE PANCAKES WITH CREAM CHEESE AND SMOKED SALMON

These potato pancakes are delicious with all sorts of toppings, but smoked salmon is my favourite. I've made four large ones but you could make lots of smaller ones if you prefer and just put a little pile of salmon on top of the cream cheese. They also make a great cold addition to a lunch box.

**Serves 4**

**1 large all-purpose potato, such as Maris Piper, about 250g, peeled and trimmed flat both ends**
**4 eggs**
**a good grating of fresh nutmeg**
**30g Parmesan cheese, freshly grated**
**salt and freshly ground black pepper**
**4 tbsp olive oil**
**4 heaped tbsp cream cheese (or low-fat soft white cheese)**
**120g pack smoked salmon trimmings**

***To serve***
**lemon wedges**

1. Spiralize the potato on the 5mm noodle blade. Snip into short lengths of about 3cm with scissors, a handful at a time. Don't worry if some are larger or smaller – just snip the pile in numerous places.
2. Boil the noodles in a pan with about 2cm water for 2 minutes until tender but still holding their shape. Drain thoroughly.
3. Beat the eggs in a bowl. Add the nutmeg, cheese, a pinch of salt and plenty of pepper. Stir in the potatoes and mix well.

4 Heat 1 tbsp oil in a 20cm frying pan and swirl so it coats the base. Spoon in a quarter of the mixture and spread out over the base of the pan to form a pancake. Fry over a medium heat for a few minutes until golden brown underneath and almost set on top. Flip over and brown the other side. Remove from the pan and keep warm while you cook the remaining 3 pancakes.

5 Quickly spread each pancake with cream cheese, then crumble a quarter of the smoked salmon trimmings over half of each one. Fold each pancake over the salmon to form a half-moon shape and press down lightly. Serve straight away with wedges of lemon to squeeze over.

# PLANTAIN BREAKFAST MUFFINS

These make a great breakfast on the go. They're packed with goodness to give slow-release energy (not for the low-carb dieters!) and will keep for days in an airtight container. If eating at home, they're particularly good served warm. If you like your muffins a little sweeter, use pure apple juice instead of milk and ring the changes with other dried fruits, such as cranberries, chopped dates or sultanas.

**Makes about 12**

**1 plantain (or totally green banana), peeled and halved widthways**
**75g dried blueberries**
**75g raisins**
**75g spelt flour**
**50g rolled oats**
**35g ground almonds**
**2 tbsp dried milk powder**
**2 tsp baking powder**
**6 tbsp sunflower oil**
**150ml milk**
**1½ tsp natural vanilla extract**

1. Preheat the oven to 190°C/Gas 5. Line 9 sections of a deep muffin pan with large paper cake cases.
2. Spiralize the plantain on the 5mm noodle blade. Put in a food processor and pulse briefly to chop finely, or chop finely by hand.
3. Place in a large bowl and add all the remaining ingredients. Mix together well.
4. Spoon the mixture into the muffin cases. It should reach almost to the top of the cases and look rough – like rock cakes.
5. Bake for about 25 minutes until golden and firm to the touch (and the bases look brown if you pick one up with an ovengloved hand).
6. Cool on a wire rack and store in an airtight container.

# SPIRALIZED HASH BROWNS

These are gorgeous for breakfast with some bacon and eggs or just a serving of baked beans or grilled portobello mushrooms. They're also tasty for lunch or supper along with grilled meat, chicken or even halloumi cheese.

**Serves 4**

**2 potatoes, about 400g total weight, peeled and trimmed**
**1 onion, peeled**
**1 egg, beaten**
**salt and freshly ground black pepper**
**groundnut or sunflower oil, for frying**

1. Spiralize the potato on the 3mm noodle blade and the onion on the wide curls blade. Put in a food processor and pulse briefly to chop finely, or chop finely by hand.
2. Put in a colander and press to squeeze out any excess moisture, then place in a bowl and add the beaten egg and some salt and pepper. Mix well.
3. Heat about 5mm oil in a large frying pan. Add spoonfuls of the potato mixture and flatten to form cakes. Fry for about 3 minutes on each side until crisp, golden and cooked through. Drain on kitchen paper and serve hot.

# CELERIAC AND SMOKED HADDOCK KEDGEREE

Celeriac makes lovely vegetable 'rice' grains – just make sure you don't cook them too much or they become extremely soft. The trick is to cook them briefly in boiling water to the texture you like, then drain straight away, and always toss through the rest of the ingredients just before serving. Traditional kedgeree has curry powder added but I also like it with only the freshly grated nutmeg – especially if I am serving it for breakfast.

**Serves 4**

**2 tbsp lemon juice**
**1 small celeriac, about 500g, peeled and trimmed flat both ends**
**a large knob of butter**
**1 onion, peeled and chopped**
**1 tsp curry powder (optional)**
**85g frozen peas**
**300g undyed smoked haddock fillet**
**200ml milk**
**4 tbsp single cream**
**a good grating of fresh nutmeg**
**salt and freshly ground black pepper**
**2 tbsp chopped fresh parsley**
**2 eggs, hard-boiled, shelled and quartered**

1. Put the lemon juice in a large bowl of cold water.
2. Spiralize the celeriac on the 5mm noodle blade. Drop the noodles into the acidulated water straight away to prevent them browning.

3. When all the noodles are made, drain them thoroughly, then place in a food processor and pulse briefly to finely chop, or chop finely by hand.
4. Bring a pan of lightly salted water to the boil and add the celeriac 'rice'. Bring back to the boil and boil for 2 minutes only, until just tender but still with some bite. Drain and set aside.
5. Melt the butter in a large saucepan. Add the onion and fry over a medium heat, stirring, for about 3 minutes until softened and only browning slightly. Add the peas, fish and milk. Bring to the boil, reduce the heat, cover and cook gently for 5 minutes until the fish flakes easily with a fork.
6. Lift out the fish with a slotted spoon, remove and discard the skin and any bones, then flake the flesh.
7. Return the milk mixture to the boil for 2 minutes until most of the milk has evaporated.
8. Add the celeriac 'rice', fish and cream, and toss gently over a medium heat until piping hot. Season with nutmeg, salt (if necessary) and plenty of pepper. Stir in the parsley.
9. Spoon onto warm plates and garnish each one with two quarters of hard-boiled egg.

# CHAPTER 4
# SOUPS AND STARTERS

Most of these soups and starters are also substantial enough to serve as a light lunch or supper as well as making wonderful openings to more formal meals. When you've added the noodles to soups, it's up to you how long you cook them. For most, I like them properly soft as they are easier to eat and all the flavours mingle comfortingly, but Asian-style dishes, such as Miso Soup (see page 25), are exceptions, as there should still be a hint of crispness to them.

# MISO SOUP

To turn this into a more substantial dish you can add some cubes of firm tofu or salmon or a handful of raw prawns and simmer for 2–3 minutes before adding the miso paste.

**Serves 4**

**2 heaped tbsp dried shiitake mushrooms**
**4 tbsp boiling water**
**1 large carrot, about 175g, peeled and halved widthways**
**1 large courgette, about 200g, trimmed and halved widthways**
**1 litre chicken or vegetable stock**
**2 spring onions, chopped**
**1 tsp grated fresh root ginger or finely chopped pickled ginger (see page 165)**
**2 tbsp wakame flakes (dried seaweed)**
**1 tbsp soy sauce**
**2 tbsp red miso paste**

1. Soak the mushrooms in the boiling water for 10 minutes.
2. Meanwhile, spiralize the carrot and courgette on the 3mm noodle blade. Snip the vegetable noodles into more manageable lengths with scissors, a handful at a time (remember this is eaten with a spoon).
3. Place all the ingredients except the miso paste in a saucepan. Bring to the boil, reduce the heat, part-cover and simmer for 5 minutes.
4. Gently stir in the miso paste.
5. Ladle into warm bowls and serve straight away.

# COURGETTE AND TURNIP NOODLE SOUP WITH HARICOT BEANS AND PISTOU

This delicious, substantial soup makes a great lunch or supper that will warm the heart on a cold day. Haricot beans are packed with protein and high in fibre so are worth eating even on a low-carb diet. You can just use one can of haricot beans for a less filling soup but still with the same great taste or, for total lightness, omit them altogether.

**Serves 4–6**

**1 large turnip, about 175g, peeled and trimmed flat both ends**
**1 large courgette, about 200g, trimmed and halved widthways**
**a large knob of butter**
**1 onion, peeled and chopped**
**2 garlic cloves, crushed**
**2 x 400g cans haricot beans, drained**
**300ml passata**
**3 tbsp dry white wine or apple juice**
**900ml vegetable or chicken stock**
**salt and freshly ground black pepper**
**1 bay leaf**

***For the pistou***
**a large of handful fresh basil**
**1 garlic clove, crushed**
**40g Parmesan cheese, freshly grated**
**120ml olive oil**

1. Spiralize the turnip and courgette on the 5mm noodle blade. Snip or break into short lengths. Set aside.
2. Heat the butter in a large saucepan, add the onion and garlic and fry over a gentle heat, stirring until softened but not browned. Add the remaining ingredients for the soup except the vegetable noodles and bring to the boil. Cover, reduce the heat and simmer for 10 minutes.
3. Add the noodles and simmer for a further 10 minutes until tender.
4. Meanwhile, put all the pistou ingredients in a food processor and blend until smooth.
5. Discard the bay leaf from the soup, taste and re-season if necessary. Ladle into warm bowls and add a spoonful of the pistou to each bowl.

# NOODLE MINESTRONE

I like to add some high-fibre macaroni to this soup to thicken it slightly and give it substance, but you can leave it out if you are on a low-carb diet.

**Serves 6**

**½ small celeriac, about 250g, peeled and trimmed flat both ends**
**1 tbsp lemon juice**
**1 carrot, about 100g, peeled and halved widthways**
**1 green pepper, stalk snipped off, leaving pepper intact**
**1 onion, peeled**
**2 tbsp olive oil**
**1 garlic clove, crushed**
**400g can chopped tomatoes**
**60g frozen peas**
**1.2 litres vegetable or chicken stock**
**1 tbsp tomato purée**
**½ tsp Italian mixed herbs**
**60g macaroni with added fibre**
**salt and freshly ground black pepper**

***To serve***
**freshly grated Parmesan cheese**

1. Spiralize the celeriac on the 3mm noodle blade. Snip into finger-length pieces with scissors, a handful at a time, then place in a bowl of water with the lemon juice added. Spiralize the carrot on the same blade and, again, snip into pieces. Set aside.
2. Spiralize the pepper on the wide curls blade, then rinse the pepper and discard any core or seeds. If your pepper is not really crisp, simply cut it into thin strips instead (see page 8 for more tips on spiralizing peppers). Cut into finger-length pieces.
3. Spiralize the onion on the wide curls blade.
4. Heat the oil in a large saucepan. Add the pepper and onion and fry, stirring, for 3 minutes until softening but not browning.
5. Add the remaining ingredients, including the drained celeriac. Bring to the boil, reduce the heat and simmer for 15 minutes.
6. Ladle the soup into warm bowls and sprinkle with grated Parmesan before serving.

# CHICKEN AND PARSNIP NOODLE SOUP

If you have a cooked roast chicken and have a carcass with a bit of meat on it, you can use that here instead, but you get more meat and succulence from using a large chicken thigh.

**Serves 4**

**1 large chicken thigh**
**1 onion, peeled and quartered**
**1 large sprig of fresh thyme**
**1 small bay leaf**
**1 litre boiling water**
**2 tbsp chicken stock concentrate**
**2 tsp soy sauce**
**salt and freshly ground black pepper**
**a good grating of fresh nutmeg**
**1 short fat parsnip, about 175g, peeled and trimmed flat both ends**

1 Put everything except the parsnip in a saucepan with some pepper and a little salt. Bring to the boil, reduce the heat, part-cover and simmer gently for 40 minutes.

2. Meanwhile, spiralize the parsnip on the 3mm noodle blade. Snip into roughly 3cm lengths with scissors, a handful at a time. Place in a bowl of cold water to prevent browning.
3. After 40 minutes, lift the chicken out of the pan with a slotted spoon, then strain the stock and return it to the saucepan. Carefully remove all the chicken meat from the bones, discarding the skin. Chop the meat fairly finely and return it to the saucepan.
4. Add the parsnip noodles. Bring back to the boil, cover and simmer for 5 minutes until soft. Taste and re-season if necessary. Serve hot.

# PRAWN AND SWEET POTATO NOODLE BROTH

This takes just minutes to make and has the lovely Thai flavours of coconut, ginger, a tickle of chilli and a hint of lemon grass and lime. I like to use lemon grass paste as it gives all the flavour with none of the effort, but you can use a finely chopped fresh stalk, or a slightly crushed dried one and remove it before serving, if you prefer.

**Serves 4**

**1 largish sweet potato, about 400g, scrubbed or peeled and trimmed**
**2 spring onions, chopped**
**400ml can coconut milk**
**600ml chicken or vegetable stock**
**1 tsp grated fresh ginger**
**1 garlic clove, crushed**
**1 tsp lemon grass paste**
**½ tsp dried chilli flakes**
**1 tbsp Thai fish sauce**
**2 tbsp chopped fresh coriander**
**120g raw tiger prawns**
**2 tsp lime juice, or to taste**

***To garnish***
**a few torn fresh coriander leaves**

***To serve***
**prawn crackers**

1. Spiralize the sweet potato on the 3mm noodle blade.
2. Put all the ingredients in a large saucepan. Bring to the boil, reduce the heat and simmer gently for 2 minutes until the noodles are just tender and the prawns are pink.
3. Taste and add more fish sauce or lime juice if necessary.
4. Ladle into warm bowls and garnish with a few torn coriander leaves. Serve with prawn crackers.

# CARROT CURL AND CORIANDER SOUP

This is a broth rather than the more usual puréed soup, but the carrot curls look really pretty and the flavour is just sensational. Try serving it with warm naan bread unless you are on a low-carb diet.

**Serves 4**

**2 carrots, about 200g total weight, scrubbed**
**a knob of butter**
**1 onion, peeled and roughly sliced**
**the green part of a leek, chopped**
**1½ tsp ground coriander**
**1.2 litres vegetable stock**
**4 tsp brandy**
**¾ tsp clear honey**
**1 large bay leaf**
**salt and freshly ground black pepper**
**2 tbsp chopped fresh coriander**

***To serve***
**crème fraîche**

1. Peel the carrots, set the peeled carrots aside and reserve the peelings.
2. Heat the butter in a large saucepan. Add the onion, carrot peelings and leek tops and fry, stirring, for 5 minutes until golden (do not let them burn). Add the ground coriander and fry for 30 seconds until fragrant.

3 Stir in the stock, brandy, honey, bay leaf and some salt and pepper. Bring to the boil, reduce the heat, cover and simmer for 20 minutes. Strain and return to the saucepan.
4 Meanwhile, spiralize the carrots on the 3mm noodle blade. Add to the stock, bring to the boil and simmer for 5 minutes until the carrots are really tender. Add half the chopped coriander. Taste and re-season if necessary.
5 Ladle into warm bowls, add a dollop of crème fraîche and scatter the remaining chopped coriander over the top.

# CUCUMBER, DILL AND YOGURT SOUP

I used to grate my cucumber for this soup but spiralizing it then cutting into short lengths gives a lovely texture and is a lot quicker and less effort than grating. If you don't have fresh dill, substitute 2 teaspoons of dried.

**Serves 4**

**1 cucumber, trimmed and cut into thirds widthways**
**salt**
**2–3 tbsp chopped fresh dill**
**2 tbsp white balsamic condiment**
**freshly ground black pepper**
**300g Greek-style plain yogurt**
**300ml ice-cold milk**

*To garnish*
**4 small sprigs of fresh dill or parsley**

*To serve*
**warm rye bread and unsalted butter**

1. Spiralize the cucumber on the 3mm noodle blade. Cut into 2.5cm lengths. Place in a colander, sprinkle with a little salt, toss and leave to stand over a plate for 15 minutes.
2. Squeeze out the moisture, then tip the cucumber into a bowl. Stir in the dill, balsamic condiment, a little pepper and the yogurt. Cover and chill for a couple of hours (if you have time) to allow the flavours to develop.
3. Just before serving, stir in the milk, taste and re-season if necessary. Ladle into soup bowls and garnish with the small sprigs of dill or parsley. Serve with warm rye bread and unsalted butter.

# TWIRLED PARMIGIANO REGGIANO

Instead of a baked dish of fried aubergine, sliced tomato sauce and mozzarella, here I've lightly sautéed aubergine curls, added some passata, basil and mozzarella and grilled until the cheese melts. Simple and delicious!

**Serves 4**

**1 firm aubergine, about 250g, trimmed flat both ends**
**3 tbsp olive oil**
**6 tbsp passata**
**salt and freshly ground black pepper**
**a handful of torn fresh basil leaves**
**80g mozzarella cheese, grated**

*To serve*
**ciabatta bread**

1. Spiralize the aubergine on the wide curls blade (see notes on spiralizing aubergines on page 6).
2. Heat the oil in a large frying pan. Fry the aubergines for 4–5 minutes, tossing gently until golden and tender.
3. Preheat the grill. Spoon the passata over the aubergines in the pan, season with salt and pepper, then scatter over most of the basil and all the mozzarella.
4. Place the pan under the grill for 3–4 minutes until the mozzarella melts and lightly browns. Scatter the remaining basil over the top and serve straight from the pan with plenty of ciabatta bread to mop up the juices.

# CELERIAC REMOULADE WITH WALNUTS AND BLUE CHEESE

This remoulade has a light dressing, so the whole thing isn't too rich. It's served on large crostini – slices of ciabatta, lightly fried in olive oil and garlic – and makes a delicious starter or light lunch dish. Those on a low-carb diet can omit the fried ciabatta and serve it piled on large iceberg lettuce leaves, carefully removed from the tight head so they form perfect edible bowls.

**Serves 4**

***For the crostini***
**4 tbsp olive oil**
**1 garlic clove, halved**
**4 large slices of ciabatta, cut on the diagonal**

***For the dressing***
**4 tbsp mayonnaise**
**2 tbsp walnut oil**
**1 tbsp white balsamic condiment**
**2 tbsp snipped fresh chives**
**salt and freshly ground black pepper**

***For the remoulade***
**1 small celeriac, about 500g, peeled and trimmed flat both ends**
**60g Stilton or other blue cheese, crumbled**
**40g walnuts, chopped**

***To garnish***
**8 long chive stalks**

1. First make the crostini. Heat the oil in a large frying pan and add the two halves of garlic. When hot but not smoking, add the bread and fry over a medium heat on both sides until golden but not too crisp. Drain on kitchen paper and set aside.
2. Mix all the dressing ingredients in a large bowl, seasoning to taste with salt and pepper.
3. Spiralize the celeriac on the 3mm noodle blade. Snip into short lengths with scissors, a handful at a time.
4. Add the celeriac, cheese and walnuts to the dressing and mix thoroughly.
5. Place the crostini on serving plates and pile the remoulade on top. Cross two chive stalks on top of each and serve.

# CUCUMBER RIBBONS WITH PRAWNS

Simple and delicious, this dish is ideal when guests arrive unexpectedly. If you don't have prawns in the freezer you could use tuna instead. The fennel adds a lovely flavour and texture but you can leave it out if you don't have any. It's worth keeping a bottle of anchovy essence in the cupboard as it enhances any fish dish and keeps for ages.

**Serves 4**

**1 large cucumber, trimmed and cut into quarters widthways**
**1 tbsp lemon juice**
**3 tbsp olive oil**
**½ tsp clear honey**
**2 tsp fennel seeds (optional)**
**1 tsp anchovy essence (optional)**
**salt and freshly ground black pepper**
**200g cooked peeled prawns, thawed if frozen**

***To garnish***
**4 dollops of mayonnaise**
**2 tbsp chopped fresh parsley**

***To serve***
**toasted sourdough bread and unsalted butter**

1 Spiralize the cucumber on the wide curls blade. Place in a large bowl.
2 Whisk together the lemon juice, olive oil, honey and fennel and anchovy essence, if using, and some salt and pepper. Drizzle over the cucumber.
3 Dry the prawns on kitchen paper. Add them to the cucumber and toss everything together. Pile in small bowls, top each one with a dollop of mayonnaise and sprinkle with the parsley.
4 Serve with toasted sourdough bread and unsalted butter.

# CRISPY POTATO STICKS WITH AVOCADO DIP, PICKLES AND RADISHES

I first made this with pasta noodles but the potato ones taste sublime. The dip can be made up to 2 hours before you are ready to serve and the crispy potato sticks can be served cold too. You can vary the pickles as you wish but I find these add the best contrasts of flavours and textures. The sticks also make a great nibble with drinks.

**Serves 4**

***For the avocado dip***
**1 small ripe avocado**
**2 tbsp mayonnaise**
**a pinch of chilli flakes**
**a few drops of Worcestershire sauce**
**a squeeze of lemon juice**
**salt and freshly ground black pepper**

***For the potato sticks***
**1 large potato, about 350g, peeled and trimmed flat either end**
**groundnut or sunflower oil, for deep-frying**
**salt**

***To serve***
**baby pickled gherkins, French breakfast radishes, black and green olives**

1. Scoop the avocado flesh into a small bowl. Mash with a fork, then beat in the mayonnaise, chilli flakes, Worcestershire sauce and lemon juice to taste. Spoon into 4 very small dishes or set aside to put a dollop on each serving plate later. Chill.
2. Spiralize the potato on the 5mm noodle blade. Cut into 7.5cm lengths. Pat dry on kitchen paper.
3. Heat the oil to 190°C or until a cube of day-old bread browns in 30 seconds. Deep-fry the noodles in batches until crisp and golden brown, about 5 minutes, spreading them out in the pan with a slotted spoon so they are not tangled together, and reheating the oil between batches. Drain on kitchen paper and toss with a little salt.
4. Put a pile of the crispy sticks on each serving plate, add the little dishes of avocado dip or put a dollop on the side of each plate and then add little piles of gherkins, radishes and olives to each. Eat with the fingers.

# SMOKED MACKEREL WITH BEETROOT NOODLES IN HORSERADISH MAYONNAISE

Here I've made cooked beetroot noodles. In the salad on page 140 you'll find raw ones. Use that method instead if you prefer a crunchier accompaniment to your mackerel. Because they are cooked, they will secure easily on the spikes so there's probably no need to trim. Don't press too hard or you'll squash them! You can use a vacuum pack of cooked beetroot but do make sure they are not preserved in vinegar.

**Serves 4**

**4 cooked, peeled beetroot, 250g total weight**
**2 tbsp mayonnaise**
**2 tbsp milk**
**2 tsp hot horseradish relish**
**freshly ground black pepper**
**4 smoked mackerel fillets**
**2 tsp caraway seeds**

***To garnish***
**lemon wedges**

***To serve***
**warm wholemeal rolls**

1. Spiralize the beetroot on the 3mm noodle blade. Set aside.
2. Mix together the mayonnaise, milk, horseradish and some pepper in a bowl. Add the beetroot noodles and toss gently to coat in the mixture.
3. Lay the mackerel fillets on serving plates. Put a pile of beetroot noodles to the side of each and sprinkle with the caraway seeds. Garnish each plate with a wedge of lemon to squeeze over the fish. Serve with warm wholemeal rolls.

# YELLOW COURGETTE NOODLES WITH HOT CHILLI OIL

Yellow courgettes look particularly pretty with the flecks of red and green chilli but you could, of course, use ordinary green courgettes instead. If you don't like too much heat, omit the thin chilli.

**Serves 4**

**4–5 yellow courgettes, about 450g total weight, trimmed and halved widthways**
**6 tbsp olive oil**
**4 garlic cloves, chopped**
**1 fat red chilli, deseeded and chopped**
**1 fat green chilli, deseeded and chopped**
**1 thin red or green chilli, deseeded and chopped**
**salt and freshly ground black pepper**
**2 tbsp chopped fresh basil**

***To serve***
**freshly grated Parmesan cheese and rosemary focaccia or olive ciabatta bread**

1. Spiralize the courgettes on the 3mm noodle blade. Set aside.
2. Put the oil in a saucepan large enough to hold the noodles easily, add the garlic and chillies and heat over a medium heat for 3–4 minutes until everything starts to sizzle, but without colouring the garlic or chillies. This will develop the flavours.
3. Add the courgettes, a little salt and plenty of black pepper and toss well over a medium heat until the noodles are heated through.
4. Pile into shallow bowls and serve straight away with freshly grated Parmesan cheese and rosemary focaccia or olive ciabatta bread to mop up the delicious chilli oil and juices.

# CHILLED GREEK-STYLE MUSHROOMS ON TURNIP NOODLES

These mushrooms are also delicious hot, but the flavour really intensifies if you cook them a day in advance and chill them in the fridge. The dish can also be served as a vegetarian main course for three or four people, but in that case I usually add some protein in the form of a can of drained chickpeas to the mushrooms.

**Serves 6**

***For the mushrooms***
**1 onion, peeled and finely chopped**
**2 garlic cloves, crushed**
**4 tbsp olive oil**
**300ml dry white wine**
**400g can chopped tomatoes**
**1 bouquet garni sachet**
**1 tsp clear honey (optional)**
**500g button mushrooms**
**salt and freshly ground black pepper**

***For the noodles***
**3 large turnips, about 525g total weight, peeled and trimmed flat both ends**
**30g butter**
**2 tbsp chopped fresh thyme**

***To garnish***
**a little chopped fresh parsley**

1. Fry the onion and garlic gently in the olive oil for 3 minutes until softened but not browned.
2. Add the remaining ingredients for the mushrooms and bring to the boil, then reduce the heat and simmer, uncovered, stirring occasionally, for about 15 minutes until cooked through and the sauce is thick and rich. Taste and re-season if necessary. Discard the bouquet garni.
3. Meanwhile, spiralize the turnips on the 3mm noodle blade. Bring a pan of water to the boil, drop in the turnip noodles, bring back to the boil and boil for 1 minute until just tender but still with some bite. Don't overcook. Drain thoroughly.
4. Melt the butter in the noodle pan and add the thyme and some salt and pepper. Add the noodles and toss very gently over a medium heat until the noodles are coated and hot through.
5. Pile the noodles on warm plates and top with the mushrooms. Garnish with a little chopped parsley before serving.

# PEPPERED BEEF CARPACCIO CURLS WITH PARMESAN SHAVINGS

The trick if you want curls of beef is to make sure it is frozen for at least 2 hours before slicing. Always use top-quality meat from a reliable source, too, as it is served raw. I use multi-coloured peppercorns (often called Bristol blend) but you can use all green, pink or black if you prefer. There will be a piece left at the end that won't spiralize. As with vegetables, don't waste it. Cut it into thin strips and use in a stir-fry (see page 56).

**Serves 6–8**

**3 tbsp multicoloured peppercorns (Bristol blend), coarsely crushed**
**400g piece of beef fillet, or totally lean silverside or topside, no more than 12cm in length**
**extra-virgin olive oil**
**a few grains of coarse sea salt**
**Parmesan cheese shavings**

***To serve***
**warm rustic bread**

1 Trim the meat at the top to make it flat so the holder can connect to it properly. (Wrap this piece and store it in the fridge to go with the last bit that won't spiralize, to use in another dish.) Spread the crushed peppercorns on a plate and roll the beef in them to coat the round completely, leaving the ends unpeppered.
2 Heat 1 tbsp olive oil in a frying pan over a medium-high heat and brown the meat all over. Leave to cool.

3 Wrap tightly in clingfilm and freeze for at least 2 hours or until fairly firm but not frozen solid.
4. Spiralize the beef on the wide curls blade. Turn slowly or you will get a heap of very fine shavings. (If this happens, don't worry, put them on the plates too as they still taste delicious!)
5 Arrange attractively on serving plates. Drizzle with olive oil and scatter over a few grains of sea salt and some Parmesan cheese shavings. Serve with warm rustic bread.

# SMOKED TROUT WITH DILL CUCUMBER NOODLES

These dill noodles are just as tasty served with smoked salmon, or try them as a side salad with grilled oily fish for a pleasant change from the more usual green salad.

**Serves 4**

**1 cucumber, trimmed and cut into thirds widthways**
**2 tbsp white balsamic condiment**
**2 tbsp chopped fresh dill or 2 tsp dried dill**
**freshly ground black pepper**
**4 smoked trout fillets**

***To garnish***
**4 sprigs of fresh dill or parsley**

***To serve***
**seeded rolls**

1. Spiralize the cucumber on the 3mm noodle blade. Gently squeeze and drain off excess moisture. Place in a container with a sealable lid. Drizzle with the balsamic condiment, add the dill and some black pepper and toss. Chill for an hour or two to allow the flavours to develop.
2. Lay the fish fillets on plates with a pile of the cucumber noodles alongside. Garnish with small sprigs of dill or parsley. Serve with seeded rolls.

# CHAPTER 5
# MEAT AND NOODLE MAINS

Here is a wide range of delicious meaty dishes that all incorporate vegetable noodles, either intertwined or as a base on which to serve the meat. All the recipes are carefully balanced in terms of flavour and texture and, where necessary, they have starchy carb suggestions to serve with them to help you maintain a healthy, balanced diet.

# BRUSSELS SPROUT VERMICELLI WITH BUTTERED CHESTNUT AND VENISON SAUSAGE SAUCE

This is a good way of using those Brussels sprouts that are really too big to enjoy as sweet little whole sprouts. The dish works equally well with a savoy cabbage (see page 7 for more information on spiralizing cabbages).

**Serves 3–4**

**400g large Brussels sprouts, trimmed**
**a large knob of butter**
**6 venison sausages, skinned**
**270g can cooked chestnuts, chopped (by hand or in a food processor)**
**150ml beef stock**
**2 tbsp chopped fresh parsley, plus extra to garnish**
**salt and freshly ground black pepper**

*To serve*
**sourdough rye bread**

1. Spiralize the Brussels sprouts on the wide curls blade. Cook in a steamer or in a metal colander over a pan of simmering water for 4–5 minutes until softened but still with some texture. Set aside.
2. Meanwhile, melt the butter in a large frying pan or wok. Crumble the venison sausages into small pieces and stir-fry for about 3 minutes until browned all over and cooked through.
3. Add the remaining sauce ingredients and toss for 2 minutes.
4. Tip the sprout noodles into the sauce and toss gently. Taste and re-season if necessary.
5. Pile into bowls, garnish with chopped parsley and serve with some sourdough rye bread.

# BEEF STROGANOFF WITH PARSNIP AND POTATO NOODLES

Beef stroganoff is a quick-to-make classic. Here I've used frying steak, well beaten out so it is tender, rather than more expensive fillet (but you can, of course, use that if you prefer). The earthy sweetness of the parsnips complements the rich, savoury steak.

**Serves 4**

**2 large parsnips, about 500g total weight, peeled, trimmed and halved widthways**
**4 good-sized waxy potatoes (they may just be called salad potatoes), about 500g total weight, scrubbed and trimmed flat both ends**
**1 tbsp lemon juice**
**500g beef frying steak (or use ready-prepared stir-fry meat)**
**2 large knobs of butter**
**2 tbsp olive oil**
**2 onions, peeled, halved and sliced**
**120g cup mushrooms, sliced**
**4 tbsp brandy**
**2 tsp cornflour**
**2 tsp water**
**300ml carton soured cream**
**salt and freshly ground black pepper**

***To garnish***
**chopped fresh parley**

***To serve***
**broccoli**

1. Spiralize the parsnips and potatoes on the 5mm noodle blade. Place immediately in a bowl of water with the lemon juice added to prevent browning. Set aside.
2. Place the steak in a plastic bag and beat with a meat mallet or rolling pin to flatten all over (do this a slice at a time). Trim off any gristle and cut the meat into short finger-width strips. Set aside.
3. Heat a knob of butter and half the oil in a non-stick wok or large frying pan. Add the onions and sauté for 3 minutes until softening and only slightly colouring. Add the mushrooms and sauté for a further 2 minutes. Remove from the pan.
4. Put a large pan of lightly salted water on to boil. Meanwhile, add the remaining oil to the frying pan and reheat. Add the steak and sauté over a high heat for 2 minutes until browned and just cooked through. Stir in the onions and mushrooms and toss again. Add the brandy, ignite and shake the pan until the flames subside. Blend the cornflour to a paste with the water, then stir it into the pan and allow to bubble for a minute. Stir in all but 2 tbsp of the soured cream and season to taste.
5. Drain the parsnip and potato noodles and throw into the pan of boiling water. Bring back to the boil and boil for 2– 2½ minutes until just tender but still with some texture. Drain. Add the remaining butter to the noodle pan and heat until melted. Add the noodles and a good grinding of pepper and toss gently (they will break into short noodle lengths but that's fine).
6. Pile the buttered parsnip and potato noodles onto warm plates and spoon on the beef stroganoff. Garnish with the remaining soured cream and the chopped parsley and serve with broccoli.

# BEEF AND OYSTER MUSHROOM STIR-FRY WITH CELERIAC NOODLES

Celeriac noodles are so good because they don't need cooking before adding to many dishes. Here they're just stir-fried with the partially cooked beef so they absorb all the great flavours. I find that for large celeriac, it is best to cut it into quarters and trim the tops and bottoms of each piece flat.

**Serves 4**

**1 tbsp lemon juice**
**1 celeriac, about 700g, peeled and trimmed flat both ends**
**2 tbsp sunflower oil**
**1 bunch of spring onions**
**250g steak stir-fry strips**
**2 tsp grated fresh root ginger**
**2 garlic cloves, crushed**
**125g oyster mushrooms, cut up if large**
**225g can bamboo shoots, drained**
**4 tbsp oyster sauce**
**2 tbsp soy sauce**

***To garnish***
**snipped fresh chives (optional)**

1. Put the lemon juice in a large bowl of cold water. Spiralize the celeriac on the 3mm noodle blade and place immediately in the acidulated water to prevent browning.
2. Heat the oil in a wok or large frying pan. Add the spring onions and stir-fry for 2 minutes over a medium heat.
3. Add the beef, ginger and garlic and stir-fry for 1-2 minutes until cooked through.
4. Add the mushrooms and bamboo shoots and stir-fry for a further 1 minute.
5. Add the oyster sauce, soy sauce and then the drained celeriac noodles and toss well. Cover with a lid and cook for 3 minutes until the noodles are just tender but still with some texture.
6. Toss well, pile in warm shallow bowls, garnish with snipped chives, if using, and serve straight away.

# PORK WITH BUTTER BEANS, LEEK AND SWEET POTATO NOODLES IN SESAME SAUCE

This has delicious Middle Eastern flavours of za'atar – a mixture of sweet spices and herbs – and creamy tahini – sesame seed paste. Use the dark green leek tops to flavour stock (see page 7). I can't stress enough that your leeks must be very firm and fresh or they will separate into layers rather than spiralize and you will have to slice them into thin strips by hand.

**Serves 4**

**1 sweet potato, about 400g, scrubbed or peeled and trimmed flat both ends**
**2 fat leeks, dark green tops removed, halved widthways**
**a large knob of butter**
**2 tbsp olive oil**
**250g pork leg, cut into finger-length strips, or ready-prepared stir-fry meat**
**1 garlic clove, crushed**
**1 tbsp za'atar**
**½ tsp dried chilli flakes**
**1 star anise**
**200ml chicken stock**
**salt and freshly ground black pepper**
**2 tbsp tahini paste**
**425g can butter beans, drained**
**200g crème fraîche**
**1 tsp lemon juice**
**2 tbsp chopped fresh coriander**

*To garnish*
**a few torn fresh coriander leaves**

*To serve*
**Celeriac Flatbreads (see page 158) or other flatbreads and lemon wedges**

1 Spiralize the sweet potato on the 5mm noodle blade. Spiralize the leeks on the wide curls blade, removing any outer layers that curl up around the outside of the machine.
2 Bring a pan of water to the boil, add the noodles, bring back to the boil and boil for 1 minute only, then drain and set aside.
3 Heat the butter and the oil in the same saucepan. Add the pork and garlic and fry, stirring, for 2 minutes until browned all over. Add the za'atar, chilli, star anise and stock. Season with salt and pepper and bring to the boil, then cover, reduce the heat and simmer for 10 minutes. Discard the star anise.
4 Stir in the tahini until blended, then add the butter beans, crème fraîche, lemon juice and coriander. Taste and re-season if necessary. Finally, add the noodles and toss everything gently together – there should be plenty of sauce. Heat through gently.
5 Spoon the mixture into warm bowls, sprinkle with a few torn coriander leaves and serve with flatbreads and lemon wedges to squeeze over the pork.

# TURNIP NOODLES WITH QUICK GOULASH SAUCE

This goulash sauce works equally well with spiralized white cabbage. For hungry bods not on a low-carb diet (and instead of the bread serving suggestion), you can, as I've suggested before, cook some spaghetti (preferably wholewheat or added-fibre white) and toss with the turnip noodles. Some might say that defeats the purpose. I say it means more veg and a filling, balanced meal!

**Serves 4**

**2 large turnips, about 350g total weight, peeled and trimmed flat both ends**
**1 green pepper, stalk snipped off with scissors**
**1 onion, peeled**
**175g minced beef**
**1½ tbsp sweet paprika**
**450ml passata**
**1 tbsp tomato purée**
**150ml beef stock or water**
**1 tsp clear honey**
**salt and freshly ground black pepper**
**4 tbsp thick plain yogurt or soured cream**
**2 tbsp caraway seeds**

***To serve***
**dark rye bread and a green salad**

1. Spiralize the turnips on the 5mm noodle blade. Set aside.
2. Spiralize the pepper and onion on the wide curls blade (see page 8 for tips on spiralizing peppers).
3. Dry-fry the beef with the onion and green pepper in a pan, stirring with a wooden spoon and breaking up the lumps until all the grains are separate and no longer pink.
4. Add the paprika and continue to fry for 30 seconds, stirring. Stir in the passata, tomato purée, stock or water, honey and some salt and pepper. Simmer, stirring occasionally, for about 7 minutes until pulpy.
5. Meanwhile, bring a pan of lightly salted water to the boil and cook the turnip noodles for 2½ minutes, or until just tender but still with some bite. Drain thoroughly.
6. Pile the noodles onto warm plates and top with the goulash sauce. Add a dollop of yogurt or soured cream to each and sprinkle with some caraway seeds. Serve with dark rye bread and a green salad.

# SWEDE NOODLES WITH LAMB RAGU

Swede noodles are a great alternative to ordinary pasta as they take on a similar texture once steamed, as long as you don't overcook them! You can substitute lean minced beef for the lamb if you prefer.

**Serves 4**

**500g lean minced lamb**
**1 onion, peeled and finely chopped**
**2 garlic cloves, crushed**
**120ml red wine**
**400g can chopped tomatoes**
**1 tbsp tomato purée**
**1 tsp dried mint**
**1 bay leaf**
**salt and freshly ground black pepper**
**1 swede, about 500g, peeled and trimmed flat both ends**

***To garnish***
**freshly grated Parmesan cheese**

***To serve***
**garlic bread and a mixed salad**

1. Dry-fry the lamb, onion and garlic together, stirring until the lamb is no longer pink and all the grains are separate.
2. Add all the remaining ingredients, except the swede, stir well and bring to the boil. Reduce the heat and simmer for 15 minutes until rich and thick. Discard the bay leaf. Tilt the pan and spoon off any excess fat on the surface. Taste and re-season if necessary.
3. Meanwhile, spiralize the swede on the 5mm noodle blade. Place in a pan of boiling water, bring back to the boil and boil for 3–4 minutes or until just tender. Drain thoroughly.
4. Pile the noodles onto warm plates and spoon the ragu on top. Garnish with grated Parmesan and serve with garlic bread and a mixed salad.

# VEGETABLE SPAGHETTI WITH VEAL GARLIC AND ROSEMARY SAUCE

Ring the changes by using chopped fresh sage or basil instead of the rosemary. Use British rose veal, which comes from calves humanely reared with their mothers. You could use minced pork or minced chicken or turkey instead. All work equally well.

**Serves 4**

***For the spaghetti***

**3 large courgettes, about 600g total weight, trimmed and halved widthways**

**1 sweet potato, about 300g, scrubbed or peeled and trimmed flat both ends**

**1 large parsnip, about 300g, peeled and trimmed flat both ends**

**salt and freshly ground black pepper**

***For the sauce***

**5 tbsp olive oil**

**a large knob of unsalted butter**

**2 shallots, peeled and finely chopped**

**2 large garlic cloves, crushed**

**300g minced British rose veal**

**2 tbsp chopped fresh rosemary**

**4 tbsp pine nuts**

**a squeeze of lemon juice**

**3 tbsp chopped fresh parsley**

***To serve***

**freshly grated Parmesan cheese**

1 Spiralize the courgettes, sweet potato and parsnip on the 3mm noodle blade.
2 Bring a large pan of lightly salted water to the boil. Add the noodles, stir very well and cook for 1 minute only until just tender but still holding their shape. Drain the noodles, reserving the water.
3 Heat the oil and butter in a saucepan. Add the shallots, garlic and veal and fry, stirring and breaking up the meat, for about 3 minutes until the onion is soft but not brown and all the grains of veal are separated and no longer pink. Add the rosemary, pine nuts, lemon juice and 5 tbsp of the noodle cooking water. Cover and simmer gently for 5 minutes until cooked through.
4 Add all the cooked vegetable noodles and the chopped parsley to the veal mixture and toss gently. Taste and re-season.
5 Pile onto warm plates and serve generously sprinkled with freshly grated Parmesan cheese.

# JERUSALEM ARTICHOKE CARBONARA

This is so simple to make but such a great-tasting dish. All you do is scrub the artichokes for maximum nutrients and minimum preparation! Select your artichokes wisely – they need to be as round, smooth (without knobbly bits!) and large as possible. If you can't get Jerusalem artichokes, use a 900g celeriac instead (but you have to peel that). You can also add a handful of sliced mushrooms with the onion for an added dimension.

**Serves 4**

**1 tbsp lemon juice**
**600g Jerusalem artichokes, as large and smooth as possible, scrubbed and trimmed flat both ends**
**150g unsmoked bacon lardons**
**1 onion, peeled and finely chopped**
**2 garlic cloves, crushed**
**2 eggs, beaten**
**120ml milk or single cream (or half of each)**
**salt and freshly ground black pepper**
**2 tbsp chopped fresh parsley**

***To serve***
**freshly grated Parmesan cheese**

1. Put the lemon juice in a bowl of cold water. Spiralize the artichokes on the 3mm noodle blade and place immediately into the acidulated water to prevent browning.
2. Heat the lardons gently in a saucepan until the fat runs. Add the onion and turn up the heat to medium. Sauté for a few minutes until the onions are soft and the lardons are cooked through and browning slightly. Add the garlic and toss for 30 seconds. Set aside.
3. Bring a pan of lightly salted water to the boil. Add the Jerusalem artichoke noodles and bring back to the boil. Boil for about 1½ minutes or until just tender, then drain and return to the pan.
4. Reheat the lardon mixture until sizzling and tip into the noodles. Beat the eggs and milk or cream together and add to the pan with some salt and pepper and half the parsley. Toss quickly and very gently over a low heat until thick and creamy but don't overcook or the sauce will scramble. Quickly taste and re-season if necessary.
5. Pile in warm shallow pasta bowls and serve sprinkled with the remaining parsley and some grated Parmesan cheese.

# SPICY AVOCADO NOODLES WITH PANCETTA AND TOMATOES

This only works with slightly under-ripe avocados. The trick is to choose ones that are firmer than you would normally eat but have just a very slight 'give' when squeezed. If they are completely rock hard, the flesh will be bitter, but if they are too ripe they won't spiralize. You can top each bowl with a shelled soft-boiled egg, then split each one so the yolk oozes out.

**Serves 3- 4**

**3 tbsp olive oil**
**12 thin slices of pancetta, snipped into small pieces**
**1 bunch of spring onions, chopped**
**16 baby plum tomatoes, quartered**
**1 tbsp chopped fresh thyme leaves**
**½ tsp dried chilli flakes**
**salt and freshly ground black pepper**
**3 large fairly firm but not hard avocados (with just a very little 'give')**
**6 tbsp crème fraîche**
**a little lemon juice**

***To serve***
**toasted wholemeal pitta breads or rolled-up wholemeal or seeded flour tortillas**

1 Heat the oil in a large saucepan and sauté the pancetta and spring onions for 2–3 minutes until the bacon is golden and the onions are softening. Add the tomatoes, thyme and chilli flakes, and season with salt and pepper. Cover with a lid and leave to stand while you prepare the avocados.
2 Peel one avocado at a time. Spiralize on the 5mm noodle blade, stopping as you reach the stone. Reposition the avocado the other way up and spiralize again, then on either side until most of the flesh is spiralized, leaving the stone intact. Cut off and chop any flesh still attached to the stone.
3 Reheat the pan of pancetta and tomatoes, add the crème fraîche and stir gently until hot, without allowing the mixture to boil. Add the avocado (including any chopped pieces) and toss very gently to mix in and heat through. Taste and add a little lemon juice or more salt and pepper if necessary.
4 Pile in warm bowls and serve straight away with some wholemeal toasted pitta breads or rolled-up wholemeal or seeded flour tortillas.

# PORK ESCALOPES WITH SOURED CREAM, BUTTERNUT SQUASH AND CABBAGE NOODLES

You can use courgettes instead of butternut squash for a different but equally delicious flavour. I use panko breadcrumbs for a good, crisp coating on the meat but you could use fresh breadcrumbs if you prefer.

**Serves 4**

***For the escalopes***

**350g piece of pork tenderloin, cut into 4 pieces**
**4–6 tbsp plain flour**
**salt and freshly ground black pepper**
**1 large egg, beaten**
**75g panko breadcrumbs**
**3 tbsp grated Parmesan cheese**
**groundnut or sunflower oil, for frying**

***For the noodles***

**1 small butternut squash, about 650g, with a long neck**
**1 small green cabbage, outer leaves removed and base trimmed flat**
**2 tbsp olive oil**
**a large knob of butter**
**120ml soured cream**

***To garnish***

**a few caraway seeds, sprigs of fresh parsley and lemon wedges**

1. Make a slit in the side of each piece of tenderloin and open the meat out flat. Place in a plastic bag or between sheets of clingfilm and beat with a rolling pin or meat mallet to flatten to about 5mm thick. Alternatively, split each in half completely, then flatten to form 8 smaller steaks.
2. Mix the flour with a little salt and pepper on one plate, put the beaten egg on another and mix the the panko breadcrumbs and Parmesan on a third. Dip the pork in the flour, then the egg and finally in the breadcrumb mixture to coat completely. Place on a plate and chill until you are ready to cook.
3. Cut off the bulbed base of the squash and set aside for soup or to roast. Peel the long neck end. Spiralize on the 5mm noodle blade. Set aside. Next, spiralize the cabbage on the wide curls blade, round end towards the blade, removing outer leaves as they peel off.
4. Heat a little oil in the clean frying pan. Fry the escalopes for about 3 minutes each side until crisp, golden and cooked through. Drain on kitchen paper.
5. Meanwhile, heat the butter in a separate large wok or deep frying pan, add the cabbage and squash and toss over a fairly high heat for 3 minutes until lightly browning at the edges and softened but still with some texture.
6. Add the soured cream and some salt and pepper.
7. Put the escalopes on warm plates with the noodles to one side. Sprinkle the noodles with a few caraway seeds and garnish each plate with a sprig of parsley and a lemon wedge.

# CHOUCROUTE GARNIE

You can make this using the 'real' sauerkraut on page 160 but this quick version is perfect for any time you fancy sauerkraut rather than plain cabbage and don't have any fermenting away in your larder.

**Serves 6**

***For the quick sauerkraut***

**1 white or tight green cabbage, about 800g, outer leaves removed and base trimmed flat**
**1 onion, peeled**
**300ml cider or white wine vinegar**
**300ml water**
**1 tbsp caraway seeds**
**1 tbsp salt**

***For the garni***

**a large knob of butter**
**2 tbsp olive oil**
**6 chicken thighs**
**6 bratwurst sausages or jumbo frankfurters**
**6 pork belly slices, halved if long**
**6 juniper berries, crushed**
**2 tbsp chopped fresh parsley**
**100ml dry white wine or cider**
**100ml chicken stock**
**1 bay leaf**
**salt and freshly ground black pepper**

***To serve***

**plain boiled potatoes and mustard**

1. Spiralize the cabbage and then the onion on the wide curls blade, round end towards the blade, removing any outer leaves that peel off as you work. Mix with the remaining sauerkraut ingredients in a saucepan. Cover, bring to the boil, reduce the heat and simmer for 10 minutes until the cabbage is soft. Remove from the heat. Cover and leave to stand until the cabbage is cold. It is now ready to use.
2. Preheat the oven to 180°C/Gas 4. Heat the butter and oil in a large flameproof casserole. Fry the chicken thighs, bratwurst and belly pork on all sides to brown (no need to brown frankfurters, if using). Lift out of the casserole.
3. Drain the sauerkraut and stir into the butter and oil in the pan. Tuck in the pieces of meat. Add the remaining garni ingredients, adding a good grinding of pepper but no salt at this stage. Cover the ingredients with a double thickness of oiled greaseproof paper, then tightly fit on the lid and bake in the oven for 1½ hours until everything is tender.
4. Remove the greaseproof paper. Taste and add salt if necessary (but probably not). Discard the bay leaf, garnish with some chopped parsley and serve on warm plates with boiled potatoes and mustard, making sure everyone gets a piece of each type of meat.

# KOHLRABI NOODLES WITH CHORIZO AND CHICKPEAS

Using a pack of ready-diced chorizo makes this an easy-to-prepare lunch or supper. You can also try it with turnips or swede.

**Serves 4**

**4 kohlrabi, about 600g total weight, peeled and trimmed flat both ends**
**6 tbsp olive oil**
**1 bunch of spring onions, chopped**
**1 red pepper, finely diced**
**1 garlic clove, crushed**
**100g diced cooking chorizo**
**400g can chickpeas, drained**
**½ tsp smoked paprika**
**1 tsp lemon juice**
**salt and freshly ground black pepper**
**120ml boiling water**

***To garnish***
**a little chopped fresh coriander and lemon wedges**

1 Spiralize the kohlrabi on the 3mm noodle blade. Set aside.
2 Heat the oil in a wok or large deep frying pan. Sauté the onions and pepper for 2 minutes. Add the garlic and chorizo and toss until the oil runs from the chorizo and it is sizzling on all sides.
3 Stir in the chickpeas, paprika, lemon juice, a little salt and plenty of black pepper. Add the boiling water, then add the kohlrabi noodles and toss again until the noodles are beginning to wilt. Cover and cook over a medium meat for 1½–2 minutes until the noodles have softened but still have some bite.
4 Pile into warm bowls and sprinkle with coriander, then lay a wedge of lemon to one side of each pile of noodles to squeeze over before eating.

CHAPTER 6

# CHICKEN AND NOODLE MAINS

This chapter also gives you duck and turkey dishes so there's plenty of variety, but I hate the word 'poultry' so decided just to call the chapter 'chicken'! Feel free to swap chicken for turkey (or vice versa) in any of the recipes. You could also use skinless duck breasts instead of chicken breast. If you do, leave the duck still pink in the centre when you cook it to keep it really tender as there is no need to cook it right through as is important with chicken.

# FUSION-STYLE ASIAN CHICKEN AND VEGETABLE NOODLE STEW

This is a blend of Japanese and Thai flavours and is really a main course soup as it has lots of delicious broth, so should be eaten with a spoon. You can buy wakame (dried seaweed) flakes in some good supermarkets or Asian food shops. They can be omitted if you can't find them. Daikon (or mooli) is a long white radish available in some large supermarket and Asian shops.

**Serves 4**

**2 tbsp wakame shreds**
**2 heaped tbsp dried shiitake mushrooms**
**900ml hot chicken or vegetable stock**
**1 large carrot, about 175g, peeled and halved widthways**
**1 large courgette, about 200g, trimmed and halved widthways**
**½ daikon or 1 large turnip, about 175g, peeled and trimmed flat both ends**
**1 red pepper, diced**
**225g can bamboo shoots, drained**
**4 spring onions, chopped**
**4 small or 2 large skinless chicken breasts, cut into thick diagonal slices**
**400ml can coconut milk**
**1 tsp grated fresh root ginger**
**1 garlic clove, crushed**
**1 tbsp rice wine**
**1 tbsp light soy sauce**
**2 tbsp chopped fresh coriander**

***To garnish***
**a few dried chilli flakes (optional)**

1 Soak the wakame and the shiitake mushrooms in the stock in a large saucepan for 15 minutes.
2 Meanwhile, spiralize the carrots, courgette and daikon or turnip on the 3mm noodle blade. Snip into manageable lengths with scissors (remember, they are going to be eaten with a spoon). Set aside.
3 Add the red pepper, bamboo shoots, spring onions, chicken, coconut milk, ginger, garlic, rice wine and soy sauce to the pan and bring to the boil, then reduce the heat and simmer for 3 minutes.
4 Add the prepared vegetable noodles, stir, bring back to the boil, part-cover and simmer for a further 3 minutes, or until the noodles are tender but still holding their shape. Stir in the chopped coriander. Taste and add more soy sauce if necessary.
5 Ladle the stew into warm bowls, making sure everyone gets an equal serving of noodles and chicken. Sprinkle with a few chilli flakes before serving, if you like.

# BUTTERNUT SQUASH PASTA WITH FRIED SAGE AND CHICKEN LIVERS

You can only use the neck end of a butternut squash for spiralizing so choose one with a short bowl and long neck! Store the remaining squash in the fridge and use it to make soup, dice it and add it to the 'risotto' recipes in the book, or roast it in wedges to serve with grilled meat, chicken or fish. For starchy carbs, I've added some diced potatoes to the chicken livers as I like the texture it gives the dish, but you could spiralize the potatoes and steam them with the squash or, of course, omit them altogether.

**Serves 4**

**1 large butternut squash, about 1 kg, with a long neck**
**500g waxy potatoes (sometimes called salad potatoes), cut into bite-sized chunks**
**salt and freshly ground black pepper**
**1 small handful of fresh sage leaves**
**3 tbsp olive oil**
**30g butter**
**1 onion, peeled and finely chopped**
**500g chicken livers, trimmed and roughly chopped**
**4 tbsp dry vermouth or white wine**
**100g crème fraîche**

***To serve***
**a green salad**

1. Cut off the bulb end of the squash and set aside for another recipe. Peel the long neck thinly and halve widthways if necessary. Spiralize on the 5mm noodle blade. Set aside.
2. Put the potatoes in a pan of lightly salted water and bring to the boil. Put a steamer or metal colander on top and add the squash noodles. Cover and cook the noodles for 1½ minutes only, then remove from the pan. Re-cover the potatoes and cook for a further 5–7 minutes, or until tender. Drain and return to the pan, put the squash in the steamer back on top, and cover with the lid to keep warm.
3. Select 12 of the largest sage leaves. Heat the oil in a frying pan. Tilt the pan so there is a pool of it at one side. Add the sage leaves to the oil pool and fry for about 30 seconds until bright green, curling and crisp, stirring with a slotted spoon as necessary. Drain on kitchen paper and set aside. Chop the remaining sage leaves.
4. Heat the butter with the oil already in the frying pan and fry the onion gently, stirring, for 2–3 minutes until soft but not browned. Add the chicken livers, turn up the heat and fry quickly, stirring, for 2 minutes until cooked but still pink. Throw in the chopped sage and add the vermouth or wine, a little salt and plenty of pepper. Cook, stirring, until the liquid has reduced by half. Stir in the crème fraîche and the potatoes. Taste and re-season if necessary. Lastly gently fold through the noodles.
5. Pile on warm plates or in shallow bowls and garnish with the fried sage leaves. Serve with a green salad.

# DUCK AND BLACK BEANS WITH VEGETABLE NOODLES

Duck legs – which are usually sold in pairs – are much cheaper than breasts and here you only need two to go round for four people, so that's better still! If you have a pressure cooker, you can cook the duck in that for 20 minutes so that it is really tender. The black beans add extra protein and some slow-release carbs. If you are on a low-carb diet, increase the quantity of vegetable noodles and leave out the beans. If you can't get daikon, use turnips instead.

**Serves 4**

**2 duck leg portions (usually sold in pairs)**
**400ml chicken stock**
**2 tbsp soy sauce**
**1 large daikon, about 500g, trimmed and halved widthways**
**2 large courgettes, about 400g total weight, trimmed and halved widthways**
**2 tbsp sunflower oil**
**1 bunch of spring onions, chopped**
**2 garlic cloves, crushed**
**1 tsp grated fresh root ginger**
**400g can black beans, drained**
**6 tbsp black bean sauce**
**2 tbsp cornflour**
**2 tbsp cold water**

1. Heat a wok and brown the duck legs on both sides. Drain off any fat. Add the stock and soy sauce, bring to the boil, cover and simmer very gently for 1 hour. Lift the duck out of the wok, remove the skin and cut all the meat off the bones. Cut the meat into neat pieces.
2. Spiralize the daikon and then the courgettes on the 3mm noodle blade. Stir the spring onions, garlic, ginger, black beans and black bean sauce into the juices in the pan, bring to the boil, cover and boil for 1 minute. Add the daikon and courgette noodles, toss well, cover and simmer for 1 minute. Add the cooked duck and toss again. Blend the cornflour with the water and stir in. Bring to the boil and cook for 1 minute until thickened and clear, stirring gently ocasionally, taking care not to break up the noodles too much.
3. Pile into warm bowls and serve straight away.

# CAJUN CHICKEN WITH POTATO AND COURGETTE NOODLE CLUSTERS AND AVOCADO SALSA

I've used four chicken leg portions (the leg and thigh combined) but you could use 8 chicken thighs with skin on if you prefer.

**Serves 4**

**4 chicken leg portions, with skin**
**1 tbsp sunflower oil**
**2–3 tbsp Cajun spice blend**
**5 tbsp water**
**2 fairly large potatoes, about 500g total weight, scrubbed and trimmed flat both ends**
**1 large courgette, about 200g, trimmed and halved widthways**
**1 tbsp cumin seeds**
**salt and freshly ground black pepper**
**2 eggs, beaten**

***For the salsa***
**1 ripe avocado**
**1 tbsp lime or lemon juice**
**1 red pepper, deseeded and finely diced**
**2 spring onions, finely chopped**
**5cm piece of cucumber, finely diced**
**½ mango (or 1 peach or nectarine), peeled, stoned and diced**
**2 tbsp chopped fresh coriander**
**½ tsp dried chilli flakes**

***To garnish***
**lime or lemon wedges**

1 Preheat the oven to 220ºC/Gas 7 and oil a large roasting tin and a baking sheet.
2 Put the chicken in the prepared tin and rub it with the oil. Dust the chicken all over with the spice blend (including the undersides) to coat completely. Add the water to the roasting tin (but don't pour it over the chicken).
3 Spiralize the potatoes on the 5mm noodle blade. Squeeze the noodles over the sink to remove excess moisture and starch. Place in a bowl. Spiralize the courgette on the same blade and add to the bowl.
4 Add the cumin seeds, a little salt and some pepper and the beaten eggs, then gently toss together until mixed. Divide the mixture into quarters and place them on the prepared baking sheet in 4 tangled lumps.
5 Place the potatoes on a shelf towards the top of the oven with the chicken on one in the centre. Bake for 40 minutes until the potato noodles are golden but still soft in the centre and the chicken is cooked through (pierce the thickest part of the thigh and the juices should run clear and the flesh feel tender).
6 If there is still plenty of liquid in the pan, pop it on the hob and boil rapidly for a couple of minutes to reduce to 4– 6 tbsp (you can leave the chicken in the tin).
6 Meanwhile, halve, stone and peel the avocado and cut into small dice. Toss immediately in the lime or lemon juice, then mix gently with the remaining salsa ingredients. Season lightly with salt and pepper. Divide among 4 small bowls.
7 Transfer the chicken to warm plates and spoon the juices over the top. Put the noodle clusters to one side, garnish with lime or lemon wedges and serve with the salsa.

# SWEDE NOODLES WITH TURKEY, DRIED CRANBERRIES AND HERBS

This has a festive feel to it and is a great way to use up leftover roast turkey but you can use turkey stir-fry meat instead. If so, simply toss it in a little hot oil for about 3 minutes to cook before continuing with the recipe.

**Serves 4**

**1 swede, about 800g, peeled and trimmed flat both ends**
**a large knob of butter**
**2 tbsp sunflower oil**
**1 onion, finely chopped**
**1½ tsp dried sage**
**400ml chicken or turkey stock**
**4 tbsp dried cranberries**
**100g frozen peas**
**225g cooked turkey meat, chopped**
**salt and freshly ground black pepper**
**300g crème fraîche**

***To garnish***
**chopped fresh parsley**

1. Spiralize the swede on the 3mm noodle blade.
2. Heat the butter and oil in a large frying pan or wok. Add the onion and fry for about 3 minutes until soft and lightly golden. Add the noodles and toss well. Add the sage and stock, bring to the boil, cover, reduce the heat and cook for 3 minutes until the swede is almost tender.
3. Add the remaining ingredients except the crème fraîche. Season with some salt and pepper and toss well. Cover and cook over a medium-low heat for about 4 minutes until the turkey is piping hot and everything is cooked through. Stir in the crème fraîche, tossing well so everything is well combined but not allowing the crème fraîche to boil.
4. Pile into warm bowls, garnish with the chopped parsley and serve straight away.

# SWEET AND SOUR CHICKEN

This is such a simple dish and uses mostly storecupboard ingredients. I've used fresh chicken but you could use cooked, leftover chicken – just cut it in bite-sized pieces and add at step 4.

**Serves 4**

**2 large carrots, about 350g total weight, peeled and halved widthways**
**1 cucumber, trimmed and cut into thirds widthways**
**2 tbsp sunflower oil**
**400g skinless chicken breasts or thighs, cut into thin strips**
**1 red pepper, seeded and diced**
**430g can pineapple pieces in natural juice**
**2 tbsp tomato purée**
**2–3 tbsp soy sauce, plus extra to serve**
**2 tsp grated fresh root ginger**
**1 large garlic clove, crushed**
**2 tbsp rice vinegar**
**200g beansprouts**
**2 tbsp cornflour**
**2 tbsp water**

***To serve***
**plain rice (preferably brown)**

1. Spiralize the carrots and cucumber on the 3mm noodle blade but keep them separate. Set aside.
2. Heat the oil in a wok or saucepan and stir-fry the chicken and pepper for 3 minutes until the chicken is just coloured.
3. Stir in the pineapple pieces and their juice, the tomato purée, 2 tbsp soy sauce, the ginger, garlic, rice vinegar, carrot noodles and beansprouts. Bring to the boil, reduce the heat and simmer for 5 minutes.
4. Stir in the cucumber noodles. Taste and add some more soy sauce, if necessary. Blend the cornflour with the water and stir into the pan. Cook, stirring, until thickened and clear.
5. Serve straight away spooned over some rice (unless you are on a low-carb diet) and with extra soy sauce to sprinkle over.

# CHAPTER 7
# FISH AND NOODLE MAINS

Most of my influences came from Asia and Italy as these are the areas where noodles and fish are often married together. However, I got to thinking there was no reason why the spiralizer wouldn't work with a more traditionally British-tasting dish, hence the Golden Potato Nests with Cod and Minted Pea Sauce (see page 96) and the Tuna and Sweetcorn Supper (see page 89), which is more British than Italian!

# TUNA AND SWEETCORN SUPPER

This is an old favourite when made with macaroni or long spaghetti but here I've used butternut squash instead and, rather than make a full white sauce, I've used crème fraîche and grated cheese for a lighter texture and for quickness. For a lovely crunchy topping if you are grilling the dish – and for those not on low-carbs – mix the cheese topping with a good handful of panko breadcrumbs.

**Serves 4**

**1 butternut squash, about 1kg, with a long neck**

***For the sauce***

**300g crème fraîche**
**100g strong Cheddar cheese, coarsely grated, plus extra finely grated for sprinkling**
**320g can sweetcorn, drained**
**200g can tuna, drained**
**salt and freshly ground black pepper**

***To serve***

**rye bread and a green salad**

1. Cut off the round bulb of the squash and store in the fridge for another recipe. Peel the neck. Spiralize the squash on the 5mm noodle blade. Steam in a steamer or in a metal colander over a pan of simmering water for about 3 minutes until just tender.
2. Put the crème fraîche, cheese, corn and tuna in a pan and heat through gently, stirring until piping hot. Season to taste with salt and pepper. Add the noodles to the pan and toss gently.
3. Serve straight away, sprinkle with some finely grated Cheddar cheese or spoon into a flameproof dish, top with an extra layer of grated cheese and pop under a hot grill for a few minutes until golden and bubbling, then serve with rye bread and a green salad.

# PAD THAI WITH YAM NOODLES

The yam adds a lovely texture to this ever-popular dish. If you can't get one you can use sweet potatoes (preferably the white-fleshed ones) instead. I leave the seeds in my chilli as I like the heat, but remove the seeds if you prefer a less fiery flavour. Yams are starchy carbs but contain less than white pasta or rice.

**Serves 4**

**1 large yam, about 600g, peeled, halved and trimmed flat both ends**
**1 red pepper, stalk snipped off, leaving pepper intact**
**3 tbsp sunflower oil**
**1 bunch of spring onions, cut into diagonal short lengths**
**1 thin red chilli, finely chopped**
**200g beansprouts**
**250g raw tiger prawns**
**3 tbsp oyster sauce**
**1 tbsp soy sauce**
**1 tbsp Thai fish sauce**
**2 tbsp chopped fresh coriander**
**4 eggs, beaten**

***To garnish***
**lime wedges and handful of toasted, unsalted peanuts, chopped**

***To serve***
**prawn crackers**

1 Spiralize the yam on the 3mm noodle blade. Bring a large pan of lightly salted water to the boil, add the yam noodles, bring back to the boil and cook for 30 seconds only. (If you cook longer, they will break up when you add them to the rest of the ingredients but will still taste delicious.) Drain immediately, rinse with cold water and drain again. Set aside.

2 Spiralize the red pepper on the wide curls blade (see notes page 8 on spiralizing peppers).

3 Heat the oil in a wok or large frying pan. Add the spring onions, pepper and chilli and stir-fry for 3 minutes. Stir in the beansprouts and prawns and toss for 2 minutes to soften the beansprouts and until the prawns are pink.

4 Stir in the remaining ingredients except the eggs and toss gently until blended and heated through. Add the noodles and toss very gently again.

5 Push the noodle mixture away from one side of the wok. Tilt the wok and pour the egg into the gap left. Cook, gently stirring to scramble the egg, then gently fold it through the Pad Thai.

6 Pile in warm bowls and top with the chopped peanuts. Garnish with lime wedges to squeeze over and serve with some crisp prawn crackers.

# CELERIAC RIBBONS WITH CLAMS IN WINE AND TOMATO SAUCE

Cans of baby clams are very inexpensive and make a nutritious meal any time of year. You can substitute cooked mussels or prawns instead, if you prefer. Italians would baulk at serving Parmesan with this dish, but I love to sprinkle some freshly grated cheese over just before serving. With large celeriac I find they spiralize better in pieces (as long as you have a flat-edge top and bottom) but you can try it whole first.

**Serves 4**

**1 tbsp lemon juice**
**1 large celeriac, about 900g, peeled and trimmed flat both ends**

***For the sauce***
**2 tbsp olive oil**
**1 onion, finely chopped**
**1 garlic clove, finely chopped**
**150ml dry white wine**
**400g can chopped tomatoes**
**½ tsp clear honey**
**2 x 284g cans baby clams**
**salt and freshly ground black pepper**

***To serve***
**2 tbsp chopped fresh parsley**

1 Have a large bowl of cold water ready with the lemon juice added. Spiralize the celeriac on the 5mm noodle blade (cut into halves or quarters if necessary). Place them immediately in the bowl of acidulated water.

2 Make the sauce. Heat the oil in a saucepan and fry the onion gently for 2–3 minutes until soft. Add the garlic and white wine. Bring to the boil and boil for 2 minutes until well reduced. Add the tomatoes, honey and the liquid from the cans of clams. Bring to the boil and boil rapidly for 10 minutes until rich and thick. Taste and add a little salt and plenty of black pepper.

3 Meanwhile, bring a large pan of salted water to the boil. Drain the celeriac noodles, add to the pan and bring back to the boil. Boil for only 1½–2 minutes until almost tender but still with some bite, then drain thoroughly (if you cook them more they will break up when you add them to the sauce). Add the clams to the tomato sauce and then add the noodles and toss gently over a medium heat until hot through.

4 Pile into warm bowls and sprinkle with chopped parsley to serve.

# CREAMY SMOKED SALMON DILL AND COURGETTE SPAGHETTI

You can buy smoked salmon trimmings in small packs, which are perfect for this dish and much cheaper than buying slices and chopping them. I've added some cooked flageolet beans to add a bit of extra protein, carbs and texture but you can omit them if you prefer a totally low-carb meal. You can use 2 tsp dried dill if you don't have fresh.

**Serves 4**

**6 large courgettes, about 1.2kg, trimmed and halved widthways**
**400g crème fraîche**
**400g can flageolet beans, rinsed and drained**
**1½ tsp anchovy essence or Thai fish sauce**
**2 tbsp chopped fresh dill, plus a little extra to garnish**
**2–4 tsp lemon juice**
**2 x 120g packs smoked salmon trimmings**
**freshly ground black pepper**

***To serve***
**Parmesan cheese shavings**

1. Spiralize the courgettes on the 3mm noodle blade. Place in a steamer or metal colander over a pan of boiling water, cover and steam for 2 minutes. Set aside.
2. Tip the crème fraîche into a large pan and add the flageolet beans, anchovy essence or fish sauce, dill and 2 tsp lemon juice. Scatter in the salmon, breaking up the clumps with your fingers. Heat through until bubbling, then add some pepper and more lemon juice to taste.
3. Add the noodles and toss gently. Pile into warm bowls, sprinkle with a little chopped dill and some Parmesan shavings and serve immediately.

# GOLDEN POTATO NESTS WITH COD AND MINTED PEA SAUCE

These potato nests take fish 'n' chips to a new level! They also make great vehicles for all sorts of other ingredients – you could add some chopped cooked bacon and top with a fried egg or add some caramelised onions and top with some chopped liver or pieces of grilled sausage. Or try spooning in baked beans and topping with some grated cheese.

**Serves 4**

***For the sauce***
**250g fresh shelled or frozen peas**
**2 tbsp chopped fresh mint**
**100ml vegetable or chicken stock**
**salt and freshly ground black pepper**
**a knob of butter**

***For the nests***
**550g potatoes, scrubbed and trimmed**
**1 egg, beaten**
**½ tsp celery salt**
**groundnut or sunflower oil, for frying**

***For the fish***
**500g chunky cod (or other sustainable white fish) fillet, skinned and cut into bite-sized chunks**
**100g wholemeal self-raising or plain flour**
**salt**
**100ml cold water**

***To garnish and serve***
**lemon wedges**
**tartare sauce**

1 Put the peas, mint, stock and a little salt and pepper in a small saucepan and bring to the boil. Reduce the heat and simmer for 5 minutes, or until tender. Add the knob of butter. Tip into a blender or food processor and blend until smooth. Taste and re-season, if necessary. Return to the saucepan ready to reheat for serving.

2 Spiralize the potatoes on the 3mm noodle blade for crunchy nests, 5mm blade for nests that are crisp on the outside and softer in the middle. As you spiralize, place them in a bowl of cold water to prevent browning.

3 Drain on kitchen paper. Squeeze the noodles over the sink to remove the excess starch, then divide into 4 and shape into tangled 'nests', making a well in the centre of each one (don't worry if it's more of a ring with a hole in the middle).

4 Heat about 1.5cm oil in a large deep frying pan or wok. Fry the potato nests for about 5 minutes until golden on the underside. Flip over and fry the other side until golden. (You may need to do this in batches if you don't have a large enough pan.) Drain on kitchen paper and keep warm until ready to serve.

5 Meanwhile, toss the cod in 2 tbsp of the flour. Whisk the remaining flour with a pinch of salt and the water to a thick batter. Add the pieces of cod. Reheat the oil in the pan. Lift the pieces of cod one at a time out of the batter, drain off the excess, then place in the hot oil. Fry until crisp and golden, turning once, for about 5 minutes in all. Drain on kitchen paper.

6 Meanwhile, reheat the pea sauce, thinning with a little more water if necessary so it is the consistency of very thick cream. Place the potato nests on warm plates and pile the cod in the nests. Drizzle a little sauce over the top and spoon the rest around. Garnish with a wedge of lemon on each plate and serve straight away with tartare sauce.

# SALMON AND NOODLE BOWLS

I cheat with this dish and use two sachets of miso cup-a-soup for the broth. It works a dream and the whole meal takes just minutes to make. Spiralizing the vegetable noodles is the most time-consuming part! You only need half the celeriac so I peel just down to halfway then spiralize, wrap the remainder in clingfilm and store in the fridge for another recipe. But, if your celeriac is not perfectly fresh, cut it in half, set one half aside, cut the other in half again to form two chunks, trim the top and bottom flat, and then spiralize.

**Serves 4**

**1 small celeriac, about 500g, half-peeled and trimmed**
**1 tbsp lemon juice**
**1 large carrot, about 175g, peeled and halved widthways**
**1 red pepper, stalk snipped off, leaving pepper intact**
**4 small chunky salmon steaks, about 400g, total weight**
**2 tbsp soy sauce, plus extra for brushing**
**100g baby sweetcorn, halved lengthways then halved widthways**
**100g mangetout, halved widthways**
**1 tbsp chopped pickled ginger (see page 165 or use bought)**
**600ml boiling water**
**1 garlic clove, crushed**
**2 sachets instant miso soup with sea vegetables**

***To garnish***
**a few torn fresh coriander leaves**

1. Spiralize half the celeriac on the 3mm noodle blade. Snip into more manageable lengths. Place in a bowl of water with the lemon juice added, and set aside. Spiralize the carrot on the same blade. Snip into more manageable lengths and set aside. Spiralize the pepper on the wide curls blade (see page 8 for extra tips on preparing peppers). Snip into more manageable lengths. Place in a saucepan.
2. Preheat the grill and line the grill pan with kitchen foil. Place the salmon on the grill rack and brush with a little soy sauce. Grill for 5–6 minutes until cooked through and browned on top. Wrap the fish in the foil and keep it warm.
3. Put the sweetcorn and mangetout in the pan with the pepper and add ginger and the boiling water. Bring back to the boil and boil for 2 minutes. Add the vegetable noodles, cover, bring back to the boil and boil for a further 2 minutes, stirring once or twice.
4. Add the instant miso soup and stir well. Add the soy sauce.
5. Ladle into warm bowls and place a piece of salmon in each bowl. Sprinkle with torn coriander leaves and serve.

# SWEDE MAFALDE CURLS WITH PEPPER BAGNA CAUDA

Bagna cauda is a gorgeous anchovy sauce that can be used as a dip but is also delicious as a coating for sweet swede 'pasta' pieces. I particularly like it served with sourdough bread. Even if it is white sourdough, because it is fermented it helps the body produce 'good' bacteria, which is great for helping create and maintain a healthy gut. It is rich, so do have the suggested side salad to balance it.

**Serves 4**

**1 swede, about 500g, peeled and trimmed flat both ends**
**salt**

***For the bagna cauda with peppers***
**2 tbsp olive oil**
**1 small red pepper, deseeded and finely chopped**
**1 small green pepper, deseeded and finely chopped**
**1 large garlic clove, crushed**
**10 anchovy fillets from a can or jar, roughly chopped**
**30g unsalted butter**
**5 tbsp double cream**
**freshly ground black pepper**

***To garnish***
**a few torn fresh flatleaf parsley leaves**

***To serve***
**a large mixed salad and sourdough bread**

1. Spiralize the swede on the wide curls blade, then tear into slightly more manageable lengths. Cook in boiling, lightly salted water for 3–4 minutes until just tender. Drain.
2. Heat the oil in the swede cooking pan and add the peppers and garlic. Fry over a medium heat until sizzling gently, then stir, reduce the heat, cover and cook for about 5 minutes until the peppers have softened and the garlic is lightly golden.
3. Add the anchovies and cook very gently, stirring, until they 'melt' into the oil.
4. Stir in the butter and cream, and season to taste with pepper.
5. Tip the noodles to the bagna cauda and toss gently over a medium heat until hot through. Pile into warm bowls, sprinkle with a few torn parsley leaves and serve hot with a large mixed salad and plenty of sourdough bread to mop up the juices.

# COURGETTE SPAGHETTI WITH SALMON, HARISSA AND MUSHROOMS

This is a take on a favourite hot pasta dish I created years ago and I just love the combination of salmon, harissa, capers and pumpkin seeds. Here I've added some mushrooms and the courgette noodles, rather than the original wholemeal penne pasta, and I've tweaked the sauce a bit too.

**Serves 4**

**4 large courgettes, about 1kg total weight, trimmed and halved widthways**
**4 tbsp olive oil**
**400g salmon fillet, skinned and cut into chunks**
**100g mushrooms, sliced**
**1 garlic clove, crushed**
**4 tsp harissa paste**
**8 sun-kissed tomato pieces, roughly chopped**
**1 tbsp capers**
**2 tbsp pumpkin seeds**
**½ tsp dried oregano**
**120ml chicken or vegetable stock**
**100g cherry tomatoes, halved**
**salt and freshly ground black pepper**
**1 tbsp lemon juice**

***To serve***
**toasted wholemeal pitta breads, cut into strips (optional)**

1 Spiralize the courgettes on the 3mm noodle blade. Set aside.
2 Heat the oil in a large saucepan or wok. Stir-fry the salmon and mushrooms for 2 minutes. Add the garlic, harissa, sun-kissed tomato pieces, capers, seeds, oregano and stock. Bring to the boil and simmer for 30 seconds.
3 Add the cherry tomatoes and courgette noodles. Toss well for a couple of minutes to heat through, then serve straight away with some toasted wholemeal pitta breads, cut into strips, for a good, balanced meal.

## CHAPTER 8
# VEGETARIAN NOODLE MAINS

Whenever you are cooking vegetarian main courses that have spiralized vegetables at their centre you have to ensure there is some protein in the form of dairy produce – such as cheese, yogurt or eggs – or vegetable protein in the form of fresh beans, peas or sweetcorn, dried pulses, avocados or nuts, protein-rich quinoa, buckwheat or amaranth.

# BUTTERNUT SQUASH TAGLIATELLE WITH RICOTTA AND BLUE CHEESE SAUCE

I like to add a bit of crunch to this dish by tossing a handful of chopped walnuts into the sauce to ring the changes and to add extra protein, minerals and fibre (but then I do have a particular thing about walnuts and blue cheese together!). You can use reduced-fat white soft cheese instead of ricotta if you prefer.

**Serves 4**

**1 butternut squash, about 1kg, with a long neck**

***For the sauce***
**100g ricotta cheese**
**100g creamy blue cheese, such as Dolcelatte, diced**
**6 tbsp milk**
**5 tbsp chopped fresh parsley**
**freshly ground black pepper**

***To serve***
**wholemeal rolls and a tomato salad**

1. Cut off the round bulb end of the squash and store it in the fridge for another day. Peel the neck end, then spiralize it on the 5mm noodle blade. Place in a steamer or metal colander above a pan of boiling water, cover and steam for 1½–2 minutes or until just tender but still holding their shape. Drain and set aside.
2. Put the cheeses, milk and half the parsley in the same pan and heat, stirring, until bubbling and smooth. Season with pepper.
3. Add the noodles and toss gently to coat. Pile into warm bowls and sprinkle with the remaining parsley. Serve with wholemeal rolls and a tomato salad.

# CURRIED DUDHI AND COURGETTE NOODLES

This delicious combination makes a wonderful light lunch or supper. Dudhi (or bottle gourd) is a long, pale squash, popular in Indian cuisine. If you can't get dudhi you can make the dish entirely from courgettes.

**Serves 4**

**1 dudhi, about 500g, thinly peeled, trimmed and halved widthways**
**2 large courgettes, about 400g total weight, trimmed and halved widthways**
**1 tbsp sunflower oil**
**1 small onion, peeled and finely chopped**
**1 garlic clove, crushed**
**1½ tbsp Madras curry paste**
**250ml vegetable stock**
**1 eating apple, peeled, cored and diced**
**a handful of raisins**
**50g creamed coconut, cut into small chunks**
**2 tbsp chopped fresh coriander, plus a little extra to garnish**
**227g can sweetcorn**
**salt and freshly ground black pepper**

***To garnish***
**lemon wedges**

1. Spiralize the dudhi and courgettes on the 3mm noodle blade. Set aside.
2. Heat the oil in a large saucepan. Add the onion and fry for 2–3 minutes, stirring, until lightly golden. Add the garlic and curry paste and fry, stirring, for 30 seconds until fragrant.
3. Add the stock, apple and raisins and bring to the boil. Reduce the heat and simmer gently for 5 minutes. Stir in the creamed coconut and the coriander. Heat, stirring, until the coconut has melted and blended into the sauce. Add the sweetcorn and noodles and toss well. Cover and cook over a medium heat for 3 minutes, then toss gently again.
4. Pile onto warm plates and sprinkle with a little extra chopped coriander. Garnish with wedges of lemon to squeeze over.

# RATATOUILLE WITH FRIED EGGS

This cooks to a glorious amalgamated stew, which is perfect topped with fried eggs. You may like to serve it sprinkled with freshly grated Parmesan cheese, too. Spiralizing the vegetables is a lot quicker than the usual slicing by hand and means the veggies cook evenly and quickly. Like sourdough bread, ciabatta is fermented, so is much better for your gut than ordinary white bread.

**Serves 4**

**2–3 courgettes, about 350g total weight, trimmed and halved widthways**
**1 firm aubergine, about 250g, trimmed flat both ends**
**1 red onion, peeled**
**1 red pepper, stalk snipped off, leaving pepper intact**
**1 green pepper, stalk snipped off, leaving pepper intact**
**2 tbsp olive oil, plus extra for frying eggs**
**1 garlic clove, crushed**
**400g can chopped tomatoes**
**2 tbsp tomato purée**
**½ tsp herbs de Provence**
**salt and freshly ground black pepper**
**4 eggs**
**a few halved or sliced black olives (optional)**

***To serve***
**olive or plain ciabatta bread**

1 Spiralize all the vegetables on the wide curls blade, rounded end towards the blade (see page 8 for extra tips on preparation of peppers).

2 Heat the oil in a large frying pan or wok, add the vegetables and fry, stirring, for 3 minutes to soften. Add the garlic, tomatoes, tomato purée, herbs and a little salt and pepper and simmer gently for 15 minutes until the vegetables are just tender but still with some texture. Taste and re-season if necessary.

3 Meanwhile, fry the eggs in the remaining oil in a separate pan. Spoon the noodles onto warm plates and top each pile with a fried egg. Scatter a few black olives over, if using. Serve with olive or plain ciabatta bread.

# CURLY POTATO GRATIN

A spiralizer makes a great alternative to a mandolin for thinly slicing potatoes for a gratin. This dish makes a lovely light meal with a crisp salad or can be served as an accompaniment to roast meat or poultry if you aren't vegetarian!

**Serves 4**

**a little butter, for greasing**
**450g potatoes, scrubbed and trimmed flat both ends**
**1 garlic clove, crushed**
**120g Cheddar or Emmental cheese, grated**
**salt and freshly ground black pepper**
**300ml milk**
**200ml single cream**
**2 eggs**

1. Preheat the oven to 180°C/Gas 4 and butter a 1.2 litre ovenproof dish.
2. Spiralize the potatoes on the wide curls blade. Bring a large pan of water to the boil. Add the potato curls, bring back to the boil and boil for 1 ½ minutes only (do not overcook or they will fall apart). Drain thoroughly.
3. Put half the potatoes in the prepared dish. Scatter half the garlic, half the cheese and some salt and pepper over the top, then repeat the layers.
4. Whisk the milk, cream and eggs together and pour over the potatoes. Bake in the oven for about 40 minutes, or until the gratin is set and the top is golden brown. Serve straight away.

# COURGETTE SPAGHETTI WITH BLACK TRUFFLE SAUCE

Black truffles are expensive but a little jar will make two dishes for four people, so why not treat yourself? To store the remaining truffle in the jar, cover it with olive oil so no air can get to it, then screw the lid of the jar on tightly. Store in the fridge for up to two months. For added protein, top this dish with a poached or soft-boiled (shelled, of course!) egg, split to let the gorgeous yolk ooze out. This quantity will serve 6–8 as an opulent starter.

**Serves 4**

**4 large courgettes, about 1kg total weight, trimmed and halved widthways**
**60g unsalted butter**
**4 tbsp truffle oil, plus extra for drizzling**
**4 tbsp crème fraîche**
**3 tbsp finely chopped fresh flatleaf parsley**
**salt and freshly ground black pepper**
**a squeeze of lemon juice**
**1 small black truffle, shaved**
**freshly shaved Parmesan cheese**

***To serve***
**rustic bread and unsalted butter**

1. Spiralize the courgettes on the 3mm noodle blade. Steam in a steamer or in a metal colander over a pan of simmering water for 2½–3 minutes until tender but still with some texture.
2. Heat the butter in a pan until melted, then whisk in the truffle oil, crème fraîche and parsley. Whisk until well blended and piping hot, but do not let the mixture boil. Season to taste with salt and pepper. Add the courgette noodles and toss gently.
3. Pile into warm bowls and grate or shave the truffle over the top of each dish. Drizzle with a little extra truffle oil and shave a little fresh Parmesan over the top. Serve straight away with rustic bread and unsalted butter.

# POTATO SPAGHETTI WITH FRESH PESTO SAUCE

This is perfect comfort food – potatoes bathed in scented, nutty pesto. When time is short, you can make this using a good-quality ready-made pesto sauce, too.

**Serves 4**

***For the sauce***

**1 bunch of basil, about 40g**
**1 tbsp lemon juice or to taste**
**5 tbsp freshly grated Parmesan cheese, plus extra to serve**
**1 garlic clove, chopped**
**75g pine nuts**
**90ml extra-virgin olive oil**
**salt and freshly ground black pepper**

***For the noodles***

**4 fairly large, waxy potatoes, about 900g total weight, scrubbed and trimmed flat both ends**

***To serve***

**a crisp mixed salad**

1. Put the pesto ingredients in a blender or small food processor and whiz to form a purée, stopping and scraping down the sides as necessary. Set aside.
2. Spiralize the potatoes on the 5mm noodle blade. Bring a pan of lightly salted water to the boil, add the noodles, bring back to the boil and cook for 2–2½ minutes, or until just tender (don't overcook or they will fall apart when tossed with the pesto). Drain, reserving a little of the water.
3. Add the pesto to the same saucepan and heat through, adding 3–4 tbsp of the potato noodle cooking water to thin slightly. Add the potato noodles and toss very gently until each strand is coated in the sauce.
4. Pile onto warm plates and serve with plenty of extra grated Parmesan and a crisp mixed salad.

# TURNIP SPAGHETTI WITH TOMATO AND BASIL SAUCE

This sauce can be used wherever you need a tomato sauce, but it works particularly well with turnip spaghetti – and it's good with courgette too. In summer, use 450g fresh, ripe tomatoes, but for this recipe I've used a can of chopped ones so it can be made all year round. I've used dried basil, too, so it's a storecupboard standby, but you could use 1–2 tbsp chopped fresh basil if you prefer.

**Serves 4**

**4 large turnips, about 700g total weight, peeled and trimmed flat both ends**
**3 tbsp olive oil**
**1 onion, peeled and finely chopped**
**1 garlic clove, crushed**
**400g can chopped tomatoes**
**2 tbsp tomato purée**
**½ tsp clear honey**
**½ tsp dried basil**
**salt and freshly ground black pepper**

***To serve***
**freshly grated Parmesan cheese, a crisp green salad and wholegrain bread**

1. Spiralize the turnips on the 3mm noodle blade. Set aside.
2. Heat 2 tbsp of the oil in a saucepan. Add the onion and garlic and fry gently, stirring, for 2 minutes to soften slightly.
3. Add the can of tomatoes, the tomato purée, honey and basil and season with salt and pepper. Bring to the boil, reduce the heat and simmer for 5 minutes until pulpy. Taste and re-season if necessary.
4. Meanwhile, bring a large pan of lightly salted water to the boil, drop in the turnip noodles, bring back to the boil and boil for 1½ minutes only. Drain and return the noodles to the pan. Add the remaining 1 tbsp oil and plenty of black pepper and toss gently. Pile onto warm plates and spoon the tomato sauce on top. Serve with plenty of grated Parmesan to sprinkle over, a crisp green salad and some fresh wholegrain bread.

# WARM CARROT CURLS WITH FETA RAISINS AND TOASTED PINE NUTS

This has a lovely Middle Eastern flavour, which makes a delicious change from the more usual Mediterranean influences. Serve it as a main course, or in smaller portions as a colourful starter. If you don't have za'atar (though I recommend you buy a small pot of this herb and spice blend as it's so versatile), you can use a mixture of dried oregano and ground cumin instead.

**Serves 4**

**4–6 large carrots, about 700–900g total weight, peeled and halved widthways**
**4 tbsp olive oil**
**1 tbsp lemon juice**
**1 tsp clear honey**
**2 tsp za'atar**
**100g feta cheese, crumbled**
**60g raisins**
**60g stoned black olives, halved**
**60g pine nuts, toasted**
**a handful of torn fresh coriander leaves**
**salt and freshly ground black pepper**

1 Spiralize the carrots on the wide curls blade. Bring a large pan of lightly salted water to the boil and boil the carrot curls for 2 minutes. Drain and return to the saucepan.
2 Whisk the oil, lemon juice and honey together. Pour over the carrots and add all the remaining ingredients. Toss gently until the cheese is slightly softening. Taste and add more salt and pepper, if necessary (remember the feta is salty). Pile onto warm plates and serve straight away.

# COURGETTE NOODLE QUICHE

Spiralizing the courgettes gives a wonderful texture and attractive appearance to a quiche and makes it very quick to prepare – especially if you use ready-made pastry! But you can make your own, of course, if you prefer.

**Serves 4**

**a little butter, for greasing**
**225g ready-made shortcrust pastry**
**1 large courgette, about 250g, trimmed and halved widthways**
**10 sun-kissed tomato pieces in oil, drained and roughly chopped**
**a handful of basil leaves, shredded**
**100g Cheddar cheese, grated**
**salt and freshly ground black pepper**
**150ml single cream**
**150ml milk**
**2 eggs**
**4 baby plum tomatoes, halved lengthways**

1. Preheat the oven to 190°C/Gas 5, grease a 20cm flan dish and place a baking sheet in the oven to heat. Roll out the pastry and use to line the prepared flan dish.
2. Spiralize the courgette on the 3mm noodle blade. Place in the pastry-lined dish.
3. Cut the sun-kissed tomatoes into small pieces and tuck in among the courgettes so they are evenly dispersed. Sprinkle with the basil. Scatter the cheese over the top, then season well with salt and pepper.
4. Beat the cream, milk and eggs together with a little more seasoning. Pour into the quiche. Bake in the oven for about 40 minutes or until golden, set and the courgettes are tender. Serve warm or cold.

# STIR-FRIED VEGETABLE NOODLES WITH HOISIN SAUCE, SOYA BEANS AND QUINOA

This is a delicious, quick-to-make veggie supper. I like to cook the quinoa in stock but you can use water if you prefer. For those on a low-carb diet, quinoa is a great option. It has about half the carbs of couscous and is a complete protein too (that means it has all the amino acids we need whereas most vegetable proteins do not).

**Serves 4**

**225g quinoa**
**500ml vegetable stock**
**1 large courgette, about 250g, trimmed and halved widthways**
**1 large carrot, about 175g, peeled and halved widthways**
**1 green eating apple, stalk removed**
**1 head of broccoli, about 300g, with a long stalk**
**2 tbsp sunflower oil**
**1 bunch of spring onions, cut into short lengths**
**200g frozen soya (edamame) beans**
**100g shiitake mushrooms, sliced**
**2 garlic cloves, crushed**
**1 tsp grated fresh root ginger**
**4 tbsp hoisin sauce**
**3 tbsp soy sauce, plus extra to serve**
**200g beansprouts**
**120ml vegetable stock**

1. First, cook the quinoa in the boiling stock for about 15 minutes until the grains have swollen, are tender and each one has sprouted a little 'tail'. Strain off any remaining liquid. Cover and keep warm.
2. Spiralize the courgette, carrot and apple on the 3mm noodle blade and set aside. Discard any apple pips.
3. Cut the thick stalk off the broccoli, peel it with a potato peeler or sharp knife, then spiralize on the 3mm noodle blade and add to the other noodles. Cut the broccoli head into tiny florets.
4. Heat the oil in a large wok. Add the spring onions, broccoli florets and edamame beans and stir-fry for 4 minutes. Add the mushrooms and stir fry a further 2 minutes. Add the garlic, ginger, hoisin, soy sauce, beansprouts and stock and cook for 2 minutes.
5. Add all the noodles, toss well to coat in the sauce, cover and cook for 2–3 minutes, or until cooked to your liking.
6. Spoon some quinoa into four warm bowls and top with the vegetable mixture. Serve straight away with extra soy sauce to sprinkle over.

# BROCCOLI TREE AND SWEDE NOODLES WITH SATAY SAUCE

Making broccoli into noodles is a great way of using the stumps that you may often throw away. You then cut up the florets into small pieces and add to the pan at the same time. Make sure you buy a broccoli head that looks like a tree with a long trunk!

**Serves 4**

**1 large head of broccoli, about 400g, with a long stalk**
**1 swede, about 600g, peeled and trimmed flat both ends**
**salt**
**a knob of butter**
**2 tbsp chopped fresh coriander**

***For the satay sauce***
**250ml water**
**2 spring onions, finely chopped**
**8 tbsp smooth peanut butter**
**1 tbsp clear honey**
**2 tbsp soy sauce, plus extra to serve**
**½ tsp chilli powder or to taste**

***To garnish***
**a handful of roughly chopped roasted peanuts**
**lemon or lime wedges**

***To serve***
**rice crackers (optional)**

1. Cut the thick central stalk off the broccoli and peel with a potato peeler or sharp knife. Spiralize on the 3mm noodle blade. Cut the broccoli head into tiny florets and set aside. Spiralize the swede on the same blade. Set aside.
2. Make the sauce. Put all the ingredients in a saucepan and heat through, stirring, until bubbling and the consistency of double cream.
3. Bring a saucepan of water to the boil and drop in the swede noodles. Bring back to the boil and boil for 1 minute. Add the broccoli florets and noodles. Boil for a further 3 minutes or until just tender, then drain thoroughly and return to the pan.
4. Reheat the satay sauce, adding a little water so it is the consistency of pouring cream and will coat the vegetables. Add to the noodles and broccoli with half the coriander and toss very gently over a medium heat until coated.
5. Pile into warm bowls, sprinkle with the chopped nuts and remaining coriander and lay a lemon or lime wedge in each bowl to squeeze over. Serve straight away, perhaps with some rice crackers to munch alongside and extra soy sauce to sprinkle over.

# COURGETTE NOODLES WITH SUN-KISSED TOMATOES KALAMATA OLIVES AND GRIDDLED HALLOUMI

I love this as it's so easy to put together and has many of the flavours one associates with simple Greek cooking. Serve it with some toasted pitta breads and a crisp green side salad. I sometimes use za'atar instead of oregano in this dish – although not Greek, the flavour works beautifully.

**Serves 4**

**6 large courgettes, about 1.5kg total weight, trimmed and halved widthways**
**30g butter**
**3 tbsp olive oil, plus extra for grilling**
**3 tbsp chopped fresh parsley**
**3 tbsp chopped fresh mint**
**75g sun-kissed tomatoes in oil, drained and 3 tbsp oil reserved, then roughly chopped**
**75g stoned kalamata olives, halved**
**a good squeeze of lemon juice**
**salt and freshly ground black pepper**
**250g block halloumi cheese, cut into 8 slices**
**3 tsp dried oregano**

1. Spiralize the courgettes on the 5mm noodle blade. Bring a large pan of water to the boil, add the noodles, bring back to the boil and cook for 1 minute. Drain in a colander and set aside.
2. Add the butter to the same pan and heat until melted. Add the olive oil, herbs, tomatoes, tomato oil, olives and lemon juice and heat through gently. Add the cooked noodles and toss gently, seasoning to taste with salt and pepper.
3. Meanwhile, heat a griddle pan. Oil the pan (to prevent the cheeses sticking). Coat the halloumi in olive oil and sprinkle both sides using 2 tsp of the oregano. When the pan is really hot, griddle the cheese for 2 minutes each side until striped brown.
4. Pile the noodles into warm shallow bowls and top each one with 2 slices of halloumi. Drizzle with a little more olive oil and dust with the remaining oregano. Serve straight away.

# CHAPTER 9
# MAINS WITH 'GRAINS'

There's a couple of simple tricks with all these 'grain' recipes. First, if not chopping by hand (and why would you if you have a food processor?), always pulse the noodles in the machine to chop them rather than just running it full pelt as you have more control and the whole lot will chop to an even size rather than the noodles at the base being pulverised whilst the top remains in strands. Secondly – and probably even more importantly – do not overcook them. In some dishes, you can use them raw, just tossed through the other ingredients for a few minutes; in others, you cook them only very briefly so they retain plenty of texture. As with rice, if you overcook the vegetables they will just turn to mush.

# CELERIAC ORZOTTO WITH BUTTERNUT SQUASH AND FETA

This is a great way to use up the round end of a butternut squash you can't spiralize as it's chopped and added to the dish rather than being the 'grain' part of it. The quantity isn't vital either so just use the bulb of any size you have.

**Serves 4**

**1 quantity Creamy Celeriac and Barley 'Risotto' (see page 152)**
**the round end of a butternut squash, about 400g, peeled, deseeded and diced**
**100g frozen peas**
**120g feta cheese, diced**
**2 tbsp chopped fresh mint**
**salt and freshly ground black pepper**

1. While the 'risotto' is cooking, steam the squash in a covered steamer or metal colander over the saucepan for about 10 minutes until tender. Set aside.
2. Add the peas to the 'risotto' at the same time as the celeriac.
3. When cooked, gently fold through the feta, mint and cooked squash, taking care not to break up the squash too much. Taste and further season if necessary. Pile into warm bowls and serve straight away.

# MUSHROOM AND CELERIAC 'RISOTTO'

The earthiness of the mushrooms goes really well with celeriac in the non-grain risotto. If you want to make it more substantial, cook 100g pearl barley and stir it in at the end with the cooked celeriac.

**Serves 4**

**2 tbsp dried porcini mushrooms**
**4 tbsp boiling water**
**1 celeriac, about 700g, peeled and trimmed flat both ends**
**1 tbsp lemon juice**
**a large knob of butter**
**1 tbsp olive oil**
**1 onion, peeled and finely chopped**
**1 garlic clove, crushed**
**150g chestnut mushrooms, sliced**
**250ml chicken or vegetable stock**
**3 tbsp pine nuts, toasted**
**1 tbsp chopped fresh thyme**
**salt and freshly ground black pepper**
**4 tbsp double cream**

***To serve***
**Parmesan cheese shavings, wholegrain bread and a green salad**

1. Soak the dried mushrooms in the boiling water for 15 minutes, then roughly chop, if necessary, reserving any liquid.
2. Spiralize the celeriac on the 5mm noodle blade, then pop in a food processor and pulse briefly to chop finely or chop by hand. Place in a bowl of cold water with the lemon juice added to prevent browning.
3. Heat the butter and oil in a saucepan and add the onion and garlic. Fry gently, stirring, for 3 minutes until softened but not browned.
4. Add the chestnut mushrooms and fry, stirring, for a further 1–2 minutes.
5. Add the dried mushrooms and their liquid, the stock, pine nuts, thyme and a little salt and pepper and bring to the boil. Reduce the heat and simmer for 5 minutes.
6. Drain the celeriac and add to the pan, then stir well and bring back to the boil. Reduce the heat, cover and cook for a further 2 minutes until softened but still with a little texture. Remove the lid and boil rapidly for about 2 minutes until the liquid has almost evaporated. Stir in the cream. Taste and re-season if necessary.
7. Serve in warm bowls with some Parmesan shavings scattered over, and with some wholegrain bread and a green salad.

# LAMB BIRYANI WITH TURNIP 'RICE'

Lamb and turnips are always a great combination, and they work particularly well together in this Indian-inspired dish. However, you can use swede for an equally delicious result. You could also serve this with the Cucumber Raita on page 159.

**Serves 4**

**4 large turnips, about 700g total weight, peeled and trimmed flat both ends**
**2 large onions, peeled**
**2 tbsp sunflower oil**
**450g lamb neck fillets, diced**
**1 tsp grated fresh root ginger**
**2 garlic cloves, crushed**
**¼ tsp chilli powder**
**1 tsp ground cumin**
**1 tsp ground coriander**
**1 tsp ground turmeric**
**1 bay leaf**
**175g plain yogurt**
**100ml lamb or chicken stock**
**salt and freshly ground black pepper**
**100g frozen peas, thawed**

***To garnish***
**2 tbsp torn coriander**
**2 tbsp currants**
**2 tbsp flaked almonds, toasted**

***To serve***
**popadoms, (unless you are on low-carbs), lime pickle and mango chutney**

1 Spiralize the turnips on the 5mm noodle blade. Either finely chop by pulsing a few times in a food processor or finely chop by hand. Set aside.

2 Spiralize the onions on the wide curls blade, then cut into shorter, more manageable lengths.

3 Heat the oil in a large saucepan. Add the onions and lamb and fry, stirring, for 4–5 minutes until the onions are soft and the meat is browned all over. Add the garlic, spices and bay leaf and fry for 30 seconds.

3 Stir in the yogurt, stock and some salt and pepper. Bring to the boil, reduce the heat, and simmer gently for about 25 minutes until the lamb is tender and bathed in a rich sauce, stirring occasionally (don't worry, it will curdle during cooking).

4 Meanwhile, cook the turnip 'rice' and peas in boiling water for 2 minutes until just tender but still with some texture. Drain thoroughly.

5 When the lamb is cooked, gently fold the 'rice' and peas through it until the whole thing is nicely homogenised. Taste and re-season if necessary.

6 Pile onto plates, garnish with the torn coriander, currants and almonds and serve with popadoms, lime pickle and mango chutney.

# CHICKEN-AND-CHORIZO SWEET POTATO 'PAELLA'

I love the combination of chicken and chorizo and the squid gives depth of flavour and great texture. It takes nothing like as long as a real paella to cook so can be thrown together pretty easily on a weekday evening.

**Serves 4**

**2–4 orange or white fleshed sweet potatoes, about 800g total weight, peeled**
**2 tbsp olive oil**
**1 onion, peeled and chopped**
**1 red pepper, deseeded and diced**
**1 garlic clove, crushed**
**450g skinless, boneless chicken, diced**
**120g cooking chorizo, diced**
**300ml chicken stock**
**1 bay leaf**
**½ tsp dried oregano**
**a pinch of saffron strands**
**a handful of frozen peas**
**salt and freshly ground black pepper**
**100g squid rings**
**a squeeze of lemon juice**

*To garnish*
**lemon wedges and some chopped fresh parsley**

*To serve*
**olive ciabatta and a green salad**

1 Spiralize the sweet potato on the 5mm noodle blade. Either place the sweet potato in a food processor and pulse a few times to finely chop or finely chop by hand. Place in a bowl of cold water and set aside.
2 Heat the oil in a paella pan or wok. Fry the onion and pepper over a medium heat for about 3–4 minutes until soft. Add the garlic and chicken and stir-fry for 3 minutes. Add the chorizo and stir-fry for a further 2 minutes.
3 Add the remaining ingredients except the squid, lemon juice and the sweet potato 'rice'. Bring to the boil, reduce the heat, and simmer for 3 minutes.
4 Stir in the squid and sweet potato 'rice'. Cover and cook over a fairly high heat for 4 minutes. Remove the lid and boil rapidly for 1–2 minutes, stirring occasionally, until most of the remaining liquid has evaporated. Add a squeeze of lemon juice, taste and re-season if necessary.
5 Spoon onto plates, garnish with lemon wedges to squeeze over and some chopped parsley and serve with olive ciabatta bread and a green salad.

# SPECIAL FRIED DAIKON 'RICE'

This is a delicious meal on its own or could be served in smaller portions, without the prawns, alongside Sweet and Sour Chicken (see page 86). If you can't find daikon, use turnips or celeriac instead.

**Serves 4**

**1 large daikon, about 500g, trimmed and halved widthways**
**100g cooked roast pork or chicken, diced**
**1 tsp Chinese five-spice powder**
**2 tbsp sunflower oil**
**2 spring onions, chopped**
**100g shiitake or chestnut mushrooms, sliced**
**100g baby sweetcorn, cut into thick slices**
**100g frozen peas, thawed**
**75g cooked peeled prawns, thawed if frozen**
**2 eggs, beaten**
**a splash of soy sauce**

1. Spiralize the daikon on the 5mm noodle blade. Either pulse briefly in a food processor to finely chop, or chop by hand. Put in a pan of boiling water, bring back to the boil and cook for 1 minute then drain and set aside.
2. Toss the pork or chicken in half the five-spice powder. Heat the oil in a large frying pan or wok. Add the onions, mushrooms, corn and peas and stir-fry for 2–3 minutes. Add the daikon, meat and prawns and remaining five-spice powder and stir-fry for 2 minutes more.
3. Push the ingredients to one side of the pan. Pour the egg onto the empty side of the pan. Cook, stirring and gradually drawing in the 'rice' mixture until strands of egg are incorporated through it.
4. Sprinkle with a splash of soy sauce and toss thoroughly. Serve straight away.

# GRIDDLED PORK STEAKS WITH SAGE, ONION AND WHITE CABBAGE 'RICE'

This is also delicious with griddled turkey steaks or chicken breasts. If griddling chicken breasts, make several slashes in them first so they cook through evenly. To accompany this dish, I like to cook soya (or broad) beans, then add some halved cherry tomatoes, chopped parsley, black pepper and a good spoonful of crème fraîche, then heat through gently until the tomatoes soften.

**Serves 4**

**1 small white cabbage, about 500g, outer leaves removed and base trimmed flat**
**1 onion, peeled and trimmed flat both ends**
**2 tbsp olive oil**
**4 boneless pork loin steaks**
**a large knob of butter**
**300ml chicken stock**
**1 tbsp fresh chopped sage (or 1 tsp dried)**
**150ml cider or dry white wine**
**a few drops of soy sauce**
**salt and freshly ground black pepper**

***To serve***
**fresh or frozen soya or broad beans**

1 Spiralize the cabbage and the onion on the wide curls blade, then place them in a food processor and pulse briefly to chop finely, or chop by hand. Set aside.

2 Heat a large griddle pan. Oil the pork steaks on both sides. Griddle for 2–4 minutes each side (depending on thickness) until striped brown and cooked through. Wrap in foil and keep warm while finishing the dish.

3 Meanwhile, melt the butter in a saucepan. Add the cabbage and onion and fry gently, stirring and tossing, for 3 minutes to soften. Add 150ml of the stock, the sage and some salt and pepper. Bring to the boil, reduce the heat, part-cover and simmer for 10 minutes, stirring occasionally until soft and the liquid has evaporated. Season to taste.

4 Pour the wine and remaining stock into the griddle pan, bring to the boil and boil rapidly, scraping up any sediment until reduce by half. Add a few drops of soy sauce and season to taste.

5 Spoon the cabbage and onion 'rice' onto warm plates. Put a pork steak alongside and spoon the jus from the griddle pan over. Serve with soya or broad beans.

## CHAPTER 10
# SENSATIONAL NOODLE SALADS

Most of these noodle dishes use raw vegetable noodles but there are a couple of potato ones and, of course, you need to cook them before using – just like you would if they were flour-based noodles. These are all amazing blends of flavours and ingredients and I hope they will inspire you, but remember you can throw salads together easily. Simply spiralize a couple of carrots or courgettes and mix with some nuts, seeds and dried fruit, with, perhaps, some grated cheese or drained canned pulses, add a drizzle of olive oil and vinegar and a little seasoning and you have a delicious and nutritious meal for lunch or supper just like that!

# CURLY COURGETTE EVERYDAY SALAD

This is a really simple English-style salad to throw together for a quick lunch or supper. It is robust enough to take using salad cream instead of mayonnaise if you want to be really retro in flavour!

**2 large courgettes, about 500g total weight, trimmed and halved widthways**
**2 spring onions, chopped**
**6–8 cold, cooked new potatoes, diced**
**4 tomatoes, diced**
**¼ cucumber, diced**
**4 slices ham, diced**
**3 tbsp mayonnaise**
**3 tbsp olive oil**
**2 tbsp white balsamic condiment**
**salt and freshly ground black pepper**

***To garnish***
**2 hard-boiled eggs, quartered**

1. Spiralize the courgettes on the wide curls blade. Place in a large salad bowl and add the spring onions, potatoes, tomatoes, cucumber and ham.
2. Whisk together the mayonnaise, olive oil and balsamic condiment until blended and season to taste. Add to the salad and toss gently.
3. If possible, chill for 30 minutes so the flavours develop.
4. Pile in bowls and garnish with the hard-boiled eggs.

# WARM AVOCADO, BACON, SPINACH AND POTATO NOODLE SALAD WITH POACHED EGGS

If you don't want to use za'atar, then you can use ½ tsp dried oregano, ¼ tsp ground cumin and a good pinch of salt instead.

**Serves 4**

**4 waxy potatoes about 125g each, scrubbed and trimmed flat both ends**
**salt and freshly ground black pepper**
**120g baby spinach leaves**
**1 small red onion, peeled, thinly sliced and separated into rings**
**1 large, ripe avocado, halved, stoned, peeled and diced**
**12 baby plum tomatoes, halved**
**4 eggs**
**1 tbsp white vinegar**
**4 rashers smoked streaky bacon, cut into small pieces**
**6 tbsp extra-virgin olive oil**
**3 tbsp white balsamic condiment**
**1 tsp za'atar**
**a few drops of Worcestershire sauce**

1 Spiralize the potatoes on the 5mm noodle blade. Bring a pan of lightly salted water to the boil, drop in the noodles and boil for 3 minutes until just tender but still holding their shape. Drain and tip into a large salad bowl. Add the spinach, onion, avocado and tomatoes and toss gently to combine, then divide among 4 shallow bowls.

2 Put a shallow dish of cold water beside the hob. Poach the eggs in simmering water with the white vinegar added for 2–3 minutes or until cooked to your liking. Carefully lift out with a slotted spoon and slide into the cold water in the shallow dish.

3 Dry-fry the bacon in a frying pan until crisp. Remove with a slotted spoon and scatter over the salads. Add the olive oil and white balsamic condiment to the frying pan. Heat through, scraping up any sediment and add the za'atar and plenty of black pepper. Drizzle the dressing over and toss gently.

4 Carefully transfer a poached egg to the top of each salad. Sprinkle with a few drops of Worcestershire sauce and serve.

# TOASTED GOAT'S CHEESE ON BEETROOT AND CARROT SHREDS WITH WALNUT AND CRANBERRY DRESSING

Cranberries, beetroot, walnuts and goat's cheese are a classic combination. Here they come together in a really pretty salad that takes just minutes to prepare. It also makes a great starter: simply halve the salad ingredients and use one smaller, 85g disc of goat's cheese, cut into 4 slices.

**Serves 4**

**2 large carrots, about 350g total weight, peeled and halved widthways**
**4 raw beetroot, about 450g total weight, peeled and trimmed flat both ends**
**2 tbsp walnut oil**
**4 tbsp olive oil, plus extra for brushing**
**4 tbsp red wine vinegar**
**3 tbsp cranberry sauce**
**salt and freshly ground black pepper**
**4 tbsp dried cranberries**
**4 tbsp snipped fresh chives**
**50g walnut halves, roughly chopped**
**2 Little Gem lettuce or ½ lollo rosso lettuce, thickly shredded**
**2 x 100g discs of goat's cheese, halved widthways**

***To serve***
**granary rolls and unsalted butter**

1 Spiralize the carrots and beetroot on the 3mm noodle blade. Place in a large bowl. Cut into slightly shorter lengths if preferred (though they look very pretty in the very long curls).

2 Whisk the oils, vinegar and cranberry sauce together and season to taste. Pour over the salad, add the cranberries, walnuts and most of the chives (reserving a few for garnish) and toss. Divide the lettuce among 4 serving bowls. Pile the spiralized salad on top.

3 Heat the grill. Place the 4 goat's cheese discs on oiled foil and brush with a little more olive oil. Grill until lightly browning and bubbling. Slide one on top of each bowl of salad. Garnish each bowl with a sprinkling of the reserved chives and serve straight away with granary rolls and unsalted butter.

# CHICKEN CAESAR SALAD WITH A FEW TWISTS

A Caesar salad is delicious as a main, starter or side dish and you can, of course, serve this without the griddled chicken breasts on top. Unfortunately, you can't spiralize the lettuce! Store the trimmed fennel pieces in the fridge for another dish or chop and add to the shredded lettuce if you prefer.

***For the dressing***
**½ tsp Dijon mustard**
**2 tsp anchovy essence**
**1 garlic clove, crushed**
**1 tbsp lemon juice**
**4 tbsp finely grated Parmesan cheese**
**100ml mayonnaise**
**6 tbsp milk**
**freshly ground black pepper**

***For the croûtons***
**1 garlic clove, halved**
**olive oil**
**2 thick slices of ciabatta bread, cubed**

***For the salad***
**1 large head of fennel, about 300g, top cut off, base trimmed**
**1 large courgette, about 250g, trimmed and halved widthways**
**½ iceberg lettuce, shredded**
**some Parmesan shavings**

***For the chicken***
**4 skinless breasts**
**1 tbsp jerk seasoning**

1 First, make the dressing. Whisk all the ingredients together (except salt as the anchovy essence and Parmesan are quite salty). Chill until ready to use.

2 To make the croutons, heat enough oil to cover the base of a frying pan with the garlic clove halves. When hot, add the bread cubes and toss until golden brown. Remove from the pan and drain on kitchen paper. Discard the garlic clove halves.

3 Spiralize the fennel on the wide curls blade, then the courgettes on the 5mm noodle blade for the salad. Place in a large bowl.

4 Make several diagonal slashes on the rounded side of each chicken breast. Rub all over with olive oil and dust with the jerk seasoning.

5 Heat a large griddle pan until very hot. Add the chicken and griddle for 4–5 minutes on each side until striped black and cooked through. Ideally, wrap in foil and leave to rest for 10 minutes for maximum tenderness. Place the chicken on a board and cut into thick diagonal slices, but keep each breast still in its original shape.

6 Add the dressing to the fennel and courgette noodles. Toss gently. Pile some shredded lettuce into 4 shallow bowls. Pile the dressed fennel and courgette mixture on top. Scatter with the croûtons and some Parmesan shavings, then carefully transfer a sliced chicken breast to the top of each and fan out slightly.

# FENNEL NOODLE SALAD WITH ORANGES

You need to trim the tops off the fennel as you use just the actual bulb for the noodles. Keep them in the fridge and chop to sprinkle over another salad or throw into soup. I've added some haricot beans for extra protein and starchy carbs but for a low-carb meal simply omit. I like to leave the hazelnuts whole but you can roughly chop them if you prefer.

**Serves 4**

**3 large heads of fennel, tops off and base trimmed**
**2 oranges**
**1 bunch of watercress**
**400g can haricot or cannellini beans, drained and rinsed**
**1 spring onion, finely chopped**
**12 stoned green olives, halved**
**50g toasted hazelnuts or walnut halves, left whole or roughly chopped**

***For the dressing***
**3 tbsp extra-virgin rapeseed oil**
**1 tbsp lemon juice**
**2 tsp clear honey**
**1 tsp grainy mustard**
**salt and freshly ground black pepper**

1 Spiralize the fennel on the wide curls blade, head towards the blade. Place in a large bowl.
2 Cut off all the skin and pith from the oranges then slice into rounds. Cut the rounds into quarters. Add to the fennel, including any juice.
3 Cut off all the thick and feathery stalks from the watercress and tear the sprigs into smaller pieces. Add to the bowl.
4 Add the beans, spring onion, olives and nuts.
5 Whisk the dressing ingredients together. Taste and add more lemon juice if necessary. Pour over the salad, toss gently and serve.

# CRAB AND GREEN PAPAYA NOODLE SALAD

You can buy long green papayas in Asian stores or you can use a couple of the smaller, rounder ones but make sure they are completely green and hard rather than yellow and fairly soft. If even slightly yellowing, they will be too sweet and the centre will be too juicy and pulpy to spiralize. I like to serve this with crunchy brown rice crackers (if you can, find ones flavoured with sesame seeds; they're ideal).

**Serves 4**

**1 long green papaya, peeled**
**1 cucumber, trimmed and cut into thirds widthways**
**2 spring onions, split, shredded and cut into short lengths**
**1 red pepper, halved, deseeded and chopped**
**200g can white crabmeat**

***For the dressing***
**1–2 fat or thin green chillies (according to taste), deseeded and finely chopped**
**1 tsp grated fresh root ginger**
**1 tsp shrimp paste**
**1 tbsp fish sauce**
**2 tsp clear honey**
**2 tbsp lemon or lime juice**
**1 tbsp sesame oil**

***To garnish***
**4 large iceberg lettuce leaves, carefully peeled off to form 'bowls'**
**a few torn coriander leaves**

1. Spiralize the green papaya on the 3mm noodle blade, stalk end towards the blade. When you reach the seed area, some will collect on the top of the spiralizer; scoop them away, taking care not to touch the blades (you may also need to stop and remove any seeds stuck in the blades; do this with the point of a knife but not with your fingers!). Pick out any seeds remaining in the noodles and discard. Place the noodles in a large bowl.
2. Spiralize the cucumber, then squeeze it over the sink to remove excess moisture and add to the papaya.
3. Add the spring onions and pepper.
4. Whisk all the dressing ingredients together. Taste and adjust with lemon juice or more honey, as desired. Pour about half the dressing over the papaya and cucumber and toss gently. Pile into the lettuce leaf serving bowls. Add the crab and drizzle with the remaining dressing. Scatter the coriander over the top and serve.

## CHAPTER 11

# ACCOMPANIMENTS AND SNACKS

Spiralizing your veggies make accompaniments look as if you've gone to a lot of time and trouble – it also means they cook a lot quicker! Obviously you don't want noodles in one form or another every day, but they do add interest and texture to loads of meals and, again, are a great way of increasing your five-a-day in an enjoyable way. When you don't want a 'fancy' side dish, simply prepare the vegetable noodles, cook briefly to the texture you like, then drain and either serve plain or toss in a little butter, extra-virgin olive or rapeseed oil – or why not try a nut or seed oil such as sesame, walnut, hazelnut or toasted pumpkin seed?

# SAVOY NOODLES WITH TOASTED MUSTARD SEEDS

These are delicious served alongside sausages, pork chops or steaks, or are also good as a side dish to a curry. White, green or point cabbage work equally well in this. When you spiralize a savoy you get very thin delicate curly strands. For that reason they need very little cooking indeed. One minute is enough!

**Serves 4**

**1 small tight savoy cabbage, outer leaves removed and stump trimmed flat**
**salt and freshly ground black pepper**
**a large knob of butter**
**4 tbsp rapeseed oil**
**2 tbsp black mustard seeds**
**a squeeze of lemon juice**

1. Spiralize the cabbage on the wide curls blade, rounded head towards the blade (see notes on page 7 re spiralizing cabbage).
2. Bring a large pan with about 5cm water and a good pinch of salt to the boil. Throw in the cabbage noodles, stir well, bring back to the boil and boil for 1 minute only. Drain and tip into a warm serving dish.
3. Meanwhile, heat the butter and oil in a saucepan until the butter melts. Add the mustard seeds and heat until they start to pop. Add a squeeze of lemon juice. Pour over the cabbage, add a sprinkling of salt and pepper and toss. Serve straight away.

# BATTERED COURGETTE CURLY BITS

I first had these in Greece, and they are so delicious I had to include them here. I've used beer batter but you could use the quick fish batter on page 96 instead, if you prefer.

**Serves 4–6**

**2 large courgettes, about 450g total weight, trimmed and halved widthways**
**75g cornflour**
**40g wholemeal flour**
**2 tsp baking powder**
**a pinch of salt**
**100ml lager**
**groundnut or sunflower oil, for deep-frying**

1. Spiralize the courgettes on the 5mm noodle blade. Break into finger-length pieces. Place in a bowl and toss in 4 tbsp of the cornflour.
2. Whisk together the remaining cornflour, the wholemeal flour, the baking powder, salt and lager until smooth.
3. Heat the oil for deep-frying until a drop of batter sizzles and rises to the surface immediately.
4. Add the courgettes to the batter and mix round. Take up a large handful of the courgettes in batter, separate the curls with your hands as you carefully drop them into the oil, and fry, moving around with a slotted spoon, until crisp and golden – about 3 minutes. Drain on kitchen paper and keep hot while cooking the remainder in batches. Serve hot, sprinkled with a few grains of salt, if you like.

# SIMPLE COLESLAW

Everyone's favourite salad with cold meat, pizzas, barbecues – you name it. Freshly made coleslaw is way superior to the tubs of the stuff you can buy in supermarkets, and with a spiralizer it is very easy to make. Store any leftovers in the fridge in a sealed container and use within 3–4 days. You only need half a cabbage for this recipe, but it's easier to spiralize it from the whole thing and stop when you've processed half of it. The rest can be kept for another day.

**Serves 6–8**

**6 tbsp mayonnaise**
**2 tbsp sunflower oil**
**1 tbsp white wine vinegar**
**salt and freshly ground black pepper**
**1 small white cabbage, about 500g, outer leaves removed and base trimmed flat (you will only use half this; see note above)**
**1 small shallot, peeled**
**1 carrot, about 100g, peeled or scrubbed and halved widthways**

1. Mix the mayonnaise, oil, vinegar and a little salt and pepper in a very large mixing bowl.
2. Spiralize half the cabbage on the wide curls blade, rounded side towards the blade. With scissors, snip into shorter lengths. Place in the bowl. Spiralize the shallot on the wide curls blade. Snip in small pierces and add to the bowl.
3. Spiralize the carrot on the 3mm blade. Snip into shorter lengths and add to the bowl.
4. Carefully mix everything together until blended and coated in the dressing. Store in the fridge until ready to serve.

# CREAMY CELERIAC AND BARLEY 'RISOTTO'

Lower in carbs than a full barley orzotto ('orzo' is Italian for barley), this is a mixture of celeriac 'grains' and pearl barley and has a lovely subtle flavour. It is perfect with grilled fish, meat or chicken, or you could even try it with a rich tomato-based stew. You can, of course, double the amount of celeriac and omit the barley, but this is a really good balance!

**Serves 4**

**2 large knobs of butter**
**1 onion, peeled and chopped**
**150g pearl barley**
**100ml dry white wine**
**400ml chicken or vegetable stock**
**1 bay leaf**
**a good pinch of saffron strands**
**salt and freshly ground black pepper**
**1 small celeriac, about 500g, peeled and trimmed flat both ends**
**1 tbsp lemon juice**
**4 tbsp double cream**

1. Heat a knob of butter in a large saucepan and fry the onion, stirring, for 2 minutes to soften.
2. Add the barley and stir until each grain is glistening with butter. Add the white wine and boil for a couple of minutes until it is almost absorbed.
3. Add the stock, bay leaf, saffron and a little salt and pepper. Bring back to the boil, reduce the heat, cover and simmer gently for 35 minutes.
4. Meanwhile, spiralize the celeriac on the 5mm noodle blade (try whole first but, if not, cut in half or quarters, trim flat either end and try again). Either finely chop in a food processor by pulsing a few times, or finely chop by hand. Place immediately in a bowl of cold water, with the lemon juice added to prevent browning, until ready to use.
5. Drain the celeriac and stir into the barley. Cook gently for 5 minutes until the celeriac is just tender and the liquid has almost been absorbed. Discard the bay leaf. Stir in the cream and remaining butter. Taste and re-season if necessary.

# SPICED RED CABBAGE NOODLES

This is a version of braised red cabbage that is really popular all over northern and eastern Europe. It's great with pork, bacon, sausages, chicken or veal and, actually, delicious cold with cheese!

**Serves 4–6**

**1 small red cabbage, about 500g, outer leaves removed and stump trimmed flat**
**1 red onion, peeled**
**2 red eating apples, stalks removed**
**5 tbsp red wine vinegar**
**5 tbsp water**
**2 tbsp clear honey**
**a large handful of raisins**
**1 star anise**
**1 small piece of cinnamon stick**
**salt and freshly ground black pepper**

1. Spiralize the cabbage and onion on the wide curls blade, rounded side towards the blade. Cut into shorter, more manageable lengths. Place in a large saucepan. Spiralize the apple on the same blade, stalk end towards the blade. Discard any pips, then add the apple to the cabbage.
2. Add the remaining ingredients. Bring to the boil, reduce the heat, cover and simmer gently, stirring and turning occasionally, for 20 minutes until the cabbage is almost tender.
3. If necessary, remove the lid and boil rapidly for a further few minutes to evaporate any further liquid (but take care not to let it burn).
4. Toss very gently to mix again, then turn into a warm serving dish.

# PARSLEYED POTATO CURLS

Use the largest waxy potatoes you can so you get lovely long curls, and remember to turn the handle slowly and evenly so they don't break as you spiralize. Also take care not to overcook or they will break up.

**Serves 4**

**700g waxy potatoes, scrubbed and trimmed flat both ends**
**salt**
**40g butter**
**2 tbsp chopped fresh parsley**

1 Spiralize the potatoes on the wide curls blade. Bring a large pan of lightly salted water to the boil. Drop the potatoes in the water. Bring back to the boil and boil for 1½–2 minutes until tender but still holding their shape. Drain and place in a serving dish.

2 Meanwhile, melt the butter and stir in half the parsley. Drizzle all over the potatoes and sprinkle with the remaining parsley.

# CARAMELIZED ONIONS

These are much better than chopped fried onions as they hold together in a tangle and so are much easier to pile on your steak, burger or liver or to pack into your hot dog. The trick is to cook them slowly at first until soft, then crank up the heat to brown and caramelise them.

**Serves 4**

**2 large onions, peeled**
**a knob of butter**
**2 tbsp sunflower oil**
**1 tsp clear honey**
**salt and freshly ground black pepper (optional)**

1 Spiralize the onions on the wide curls blade.
2 Heat the butter and oil in a frying pan. Add the onions and toss until coated and glistening. Fry over a low heat for 5 minutes, stirring until soft and translucent, then stir in the honey, increase the heat and fry until richly golden – about another 4 minutes. Season to taste with salt and pepper.

# CELERIAC FLATBREADS

These rustic-looking breads are delicious served with curries, Middle Eastern dishes, or even with melted cheese on top for a snack lunch! Ring the changes by using sweet potato, parsnip or courgettes (though courgettes will make them a bit stickier and you may need to slightly reduce the amount of yogurt).

**Makes 6**

**½ small celeriac, about 250g, peeled and trimmed flat both ends**
**125g strong wholemeal flour**
**125g strong plain white flour**
**½ tsp salt**
**1½ tbsp sunflower oil**
**175g plain yogurt**
**1 egg, beaten**
**2 tsp poppy or black mustard seeds (optional)**

1 Spiralize the celeriac on the 3mm blade. Cut into 2cm lengths.
2 Preheat the oven to 220°C/Gas 7 and line 2 baking sheets with baking paper.
3 Mix the flours and salt together in a bowl. Stir in the celeriac. Add the oil and yogurt and mix with the beaten egg to form a soft, slightly sticky dough.
4 Knead gently on a floured surface, then shape into 6 balls and roll out to oval shapes, about 18cm long. Place on the prepared baking sheets and brush with a little water. Sprinkle with poppy or mustard seeds, if using.
5 Bake for about 15 minutes until puffy and lightly browned, swapping the sheets halfway through cooking, if necessary. Wrap in a clean napkin or kitchen paper and leave until warm (this will soften the outsides). Best served warm (they can be reheated).

# CUCUMBER RAITA

This is usually made with finely chopped or grated cucumber, but it's quicker and eaiser to spiralize it and chop in a processor. I haven't given you the option of chopping by hand because, frankly, if you do that you may as well have grated it and chopped the mint by hand.

**Serves 4**

**¼ cucumber**
**a handful of fresh mint leaves**
**120g plain Greek-style yogurt**
**salt and freshly ground black pepper**

1 Spiralize the cucumber on the 3mm noodle blade. Squeeze the strands over the sink to remove as much excess moisture as possible.
2 Place the mint in a food processor and add the cucumber. Pulse several times to chop very finely, stopping and scraping down the sides as necessary (it only takes a minute or two in total).
3 Tip into a bowl, stir in the yogurt and season to taste with salt and pepper.

# SAUERKRAUT

This is a very basic sauerkraut. It is a proper fermented food that is incredibly good for your digestion but, by dint of needing to ferment, has to be made a month ahead of when you want to eat it. Make sure everything is thoroughly clean and the jar has been sterilised either by half-filling with water and microwaving on HIGH for 2 minutes or by boiling in a pan of water. White cabbage gives a softer result than green, so the choice is yours.

**Makes about 800g**

**1 white or green cabbage, about 800g, outer leaves removed and base trimmed flat**
**5 tsp sea salt**
**2 tbsp caraway seeds (optional)**

1. Spiralize the cabbage on the wide curls blade. Place in a bowl and add 4 tsp salt. Work with your hands, rubbing it into the cabbage until the cabbage goes limp and damp. Pack into a large wide-necked jar with a screw-top lid (such as a kilner jar).
2. Cover the cabbage with a triple layer of crumpled baking paper and press it down firmly so it weighs down the cabbage. Cover loosely with lid of the jar but don't screw it down. Lay a clean cloth over the whole thing and tuck the ends under the jar to prevent any dust getting in. Leave undisturbed in a cool room for 5 days.

3 Remove the cloth and baking paper. If the sauerkraut is not submerged in liquid, dissolve the remaining 1 tsp salt in 250ml water. Pour as much as necessary over the cabbage to cover it well. Stir the cabbage. Press the crumpled baking paper over the cabbage to prevent it floating to the surface, lay the lid on top again, cover with the cloth again and leave for a further 5 days.

4 Remove any white scum. Taste the cabbage, and if you are happy that it has fermented enough, fine; if not, re-cover and check every day until you are happy with its flavour, skimming off any scum every day. I keep mine for about 2 weeks in total before eating. When fermented to your liking, skim again, put fresh paper on top, screw on the lid and store in the fridge until ready to use. It will keep well for several weeks.

# CURLY MIXED VEGETABLE CRISPS

Spiralizing the vegetables is much easier than thinly slicing them as they really are wafer thin, so crisp beautifully. I bake these rather than fry as they're not only better for you, but I find it's easier to remove any that brown quicker than others and you do need to keep an eye on them. It is a bit of a labour of love but they do taste terrific when totally crisped. You can experiment with other roots such as carrot or turnip, too.

**Serves 4–6**

**1 potato, about 150g, scrubbed and trimmed**
**1 chunky-shaped parsnip, about 300g, peeled and trimmed flat both ends**
**1 small, fat sweet potato, about 300g, scrubbed or peeled and trimmed flat both ends**
**1 large beetroot, about 150g, peeled and trimmed flat both ends**
**1 tbsp olive oil**
**sea salt (optional)**

1. Preheat the oven to 200°C/Gas 6 and lightly oil two non-stick baking sheets.
2. Spiralize the vegetables on the wide curls blade, processing the beetroot last. Pat dry on kitchen paper. Toss the vegetables in the olive oil. Spread out on the prepared baking sheets.
3. Bake in the oven for about 50 minutes but check after 20 minutes and remove any curls that are already brown, rearranging and turning the others for even cooking, and checking every 5 minutes.
4. When all the vegetables are cooked, spread them out on kitchen paper to cool and crisp. Toss with a little salt, if using. They are best eaten fresh, but you can store any uneaten crisps in an airtight container for a day or so. (If necessary, they can be refreshed by spreading out on the turntable in the microwave and microwaving for a minute, then leaving to cool and crisp again).

# PLANTAIN CHIPS

You can use large, totally green bananas instead of plantains if necessary, but just make sure there is no hint of yellow on the skin or they will be too sweet and soft! Try adding a sprinkling of chilli powder with the salt and pepper for added flavour – or even Cajun spice blend.

**Serves 4**

**2 plantains, peeled**
**2 tbsp wholemeal flour**
**salt and freshly ground black pepper**
**oil for deep-frying**

1. Spiralize the plantains on the wide curls blade.
2. Mix the flour with a little salt and pepper in a bowl. Add the plantain curls and toss to coat. They will break up into curly rounds and a few will be smaller pieces.
3. Heat the oil for deep-frying until a little piece of plantain dropped into the oil sizzles and rises to the surface immediately.
4. Fry the plantain chips in batches (about a quarter will be enough for a batch), gently dropping them in one at a time and frying until they are crisp and yellow (they don't go really brown) and they no longer sizzle. Remove with a slotted spoon and drain on kitchen paper while cooking the remainder, reheating the oil between each batch. Serve cold. Store any unused chips in an airtight container.

# DRIED APPLE NIBBLES

These apple curls are best cut into small pieces before drying so they are easy to nibble a few at a time. Always store in an airtight container in a cool place to keep their texture.

**Makes about 35g**

**4 eating apples, stalks removed**
**1 tsp ground cinnamon or mixed spice**

1. Preheat the oven to 160°C/Gas 3 and line two baking sheets with baking paper.
2. Spiralize the apples on the wide curls blade, stalk ends towards the blade. Discard any pips. Snip into 5–7cm pieces. Place in a bowl, sprinkle on the spice and toss well.
3. Arrange in a single layer on the prepared baking sheets and bake for about 1 hour, removing any that brown more quickly. Loosen from the baking paper and turn over the pieces if necessary, then slide the baking paper off the baking sheets and place directly on the oven shelves. Bake for a further 5 minutes until richly golden and fairly crisp, then remove from the oven.
4. Leave to cool (they will finish crisping as they cool), then store in an airtight container.

# PICKLED FRESH GINGER

One would normally use sugar for this recipe but I use honey as I not only like the flavour it gives but it is a healthier option than refined sugar as it is good for the gut. Try to choose young ginger (it's not easy to tell but avoid any roots that are too fat as they will be very woody and difficult to spiralize) that is evenly thick, and divide it at logical places (where the knobs join each other).

**Makes about 150g**

**175g young fresh root ginger, peeled and trimmed flat both ends**
**2 tbsp water**
**60ml rice vinegar**
**1¼ tsp salt**
**3 tbsp clear honey**

1 Spiralize the ginger on the wide curls blade (I find that if you rewind anticlockwise every so often, then wind clockwise again, it slices better).
2 Bring a small pan of water to the boil and add ¼ tsp of the salt. Add the ginger, bring back to the boil and blanch for 30 seconds. Drain and pat dry on kitchen paper. Place in a small plastic container with a lid or a glass jar, previously rinsed in boiling water.
3 Bring the remaining ingredients to the boil and pour over the ginger. Stir gently. Cover, leave until cold, then store in the fridge for at least 2 days before using. The pickled ginger will keep for several weeks.

# QUINCE AND LEMON MARMALADE

When quinces are in season in autumn, it is really worth making a batch of marmalade as a change from quince jelly. You do have to use sugar, but for some things nothing else will do! This is delicious for breakfast on sourdough or wholemeal toast (with butter, of course!) or it's great with a selection of cheeses and some celery as an alternative to dessert (or as well as!). Using the spiralizer reduced the cooking time of the fruit dramatically. I use half granulated and half demerara sugar as I like the colour and flavour it gives, but you could use all white sugar if you prefer.

**Makes 2 small pots**

**1 large quince, trimmed flat both ends**
**1 large lemon, rinsed and trimmed flat both ends**
**250ml water**
**125g granulated sugar**
**125g demerara sugar**

1 Spiralize the quince on the wide curls blade. It is a very hard fruit so you may need to stop and fiddle a bit (see pages 6–8 for tips on spiralizing). Pick out any pips and place the fruit in a large saucepan.
2 Spiralize the lemon (make sure there is a bowl in place to catch the juice). Roughly chop, discarding any pips and the first curl if it is too thick (wrap this curl in clingfilm and store in the fridge to use to garnish drinks).

3. Place the roughly chopped lemon curls in the pan and add any juice. Add the water. Bring to the boil, reduce the heat, cover and simmer gently until the fruit is pulpy and the lemon rind is really tender, 8–10 minutes.
4. After about 5 minutes, put the sugars in a bowl that will fit over the saucepan. Place on top, cover with the lid and leave there to warm through.
5. When the fruit is soft, stir in the sugars until dissolved. Bring to the boil and boil until setting point is reached (when a little of the mixture placed on a cold plate and cooled wrinkles when pushed with a finger, or when a spoonful is lifted out of the pan and allowed to run back in, the last drop clings to the spoon in a gelatinous blob).
6. Pot in clean, sterilized jars, cover, label and store in a cool, dark place. It will keep for months.

## CHAPTER 12
# DESSERTS AND BAKES

Your spiralizer can make lovely curled pear and apple desserts, in particular (though I have used rhubarb and kiwifruit too), but it can also help to make plenty of vegetables into delicious desserts and some wonderful cakes and bakes. It can work in the same way as a grater but really is quicker and easier to use (in my opinion) and the spiralized pieces give a great texture.

# GREEN BANANA AND RYE DROPPED SCONES

If you don't want to serve these for dessert, they are delicious just spread with butter for breakfast or for an afternoon snack with a cuppa. You will probably find you need to peel the banana with a knife or make cuts down in several places then peel it off in strips.

**Makes about 22**

**1 green banana, peeled and halved widthways**
**75g rye flour**
**1 large egg, separated**
**175ml milk**
**groundnut or sunflower oil, for frying**

***To serve***
**whipped cream and blueberries (or other berries), clear honey**

1. Spiralize the green banana on the 3mm noodle blade. Either place in a food processor and pulse a few times to finely chop, or chop by hand.
2. Put the flour in a bowl. Add the egg yolk and half the milk and beat until smooth. Stir in the remaining milk and the chopped green banana.
3. Whisk the egg white until stiff, then fold in with a metal spoon.
4. Heat a little oil in a large frying pan. Pour off the excess. Drop spoonfuls of the batter into the pan a little apart and cook until brown underneath and bubbles appear on the surface. Flip over and quickly brown the other sides. Remove from the pan and dry on kitchen paper while you cook the remainder.
5. When ready to serve, top each with a dollop of whipped cream and a few blueberries. Serve three or four for a serving, with a little trickle of clear honey over the top of each.

# FRUIT SALAD CURLS

This is pretty and simple and just needs a dollop of Greek yogurt, some crème fraîche or a scoop or two of ice cream to complete. If not serving immediately, place the pear curls in a bowl of water with 1 tbsp lemon juice added to prevent browning, then just drain on kitchen paper before using.

**Serves 4**

***For the sauce***

**6 tbsp blueberry, raspberry or apricot reduced-sugar jam**
**2 tbsp water**
**a squeeze of lemon juice**

***For the salad***

**2 firm but just ripe pears, stalk ends trimmed flat**
**4 firm kiwi fruits, peeled and trimmed flat both ends**
**4 handfuls of blueberries, raspberries or blackberries**

1. Heat the jam, water and lemon juice in a saucepan, stirring until melted and bubbling; set aside.
2. Spiralize the pears on the wide curls blade, stalk end towards the blade. Discard any pips. Set each pile of curls aside separately. Then spiralize the kiwi fruits.
3. Divide each pear curls pile in half and arrange on four serving plates in an attractive pile (it should sort of resemble a flower). Gently lay the kiwi curls on top in the centre and scatter the berries over so they nestle in the folds of the curls.
4. Drizzle the sauce around the fruit and serve.

# PEAR NOODLES WITH CHOCOLATE SAUCE

Pears and chocolate are always a delicious combination. You need to toss the noodles in a splash of lemon juice to prevent them browning if you aren't serving immediately, but they are better served straight away. If you do make to use later, you will need to reheat the sauce slightly so it becomes a thick pouring consistency again.

**Serves 4**

***For the chocolate sauce***
**100g dark chocolate**
**200ml double cream**
**4 tbsp milk**

***For the noodles***
**4 firm but just ripe pears, stalks ends trimmed flat**

***To serve***
**vanilla ice cream and a little grated chocolate**

1. To make the chocolate sauce, break up the chocolate and place in a saucepan with the double cream. Heat gently, stirring, until the mixture is smooth and glossy. Thin with enough of the milk to give a thick pouring consistency. Set aside.
2. Spiralize the pears on the 5mm noodle blade, stalk end towards the blade. Discard any pips.
3. Pile the pear in shallow serving dishes. Warm the chocolate sauce again if necessary, then drizzle it over the pears. Serve topped with a scoop of vanilla ice cream and a sprinkling of grated chocolate.

# APPLE NOODLES WITH CINNAMON AND RAISIN BUTTER SAUCE

If you prefer a citrus flavour to the cinnamon, add the finely grated zest of a lemon instead. I love these with a dollop of thick Greek-style yogurt on top but you may prefer to drizzle with cream or even serve with some custard.

**Serves 4**

**4 good-sized red or green eating apples**

***For the sauce***
**50g raisins**
**4 tbsp boiling water**
**50g unsalted butter**
**1 tbsp set honey**
**4 tbsp double cream**
**1 tsp ground cinnamon**

1 Soak the raisins in the boiling water in a small bowl or ramekin dish for 15 minutes or until they are plump and most of the water has been absorbed.
2 Melt the butter in a saucepan. Stir in the honey, cream, cinnamon and raisins (including any liquid) and cook, stirring, until rich, thick and smooth. Turn off the heat.
3 Spiralize the apples on the 5mm noodle blade, stalk ends towards the blade. Discard any pips. Quickly reheat the sauce, stirring. Add the apple noodles, toss gently, pile on plates and serve straight away while the apples are still crisp.

# PARSNIP AND VANILLA 'RICE' PUDDING

This is an unusual pudding but really makes the most of this sweet and versatile vegetable.

**Serves 4**

**1 large parsnip, about 300g, peeled and halved widthways**
**400ml can evaporated milk**
**2 tbsp clear honey**
**1 vanilla pod, seeds scraped**

1. Spiralize the parsnip on the 5mm noodle blade. Place the noodles in a food processor and pulse briefly to finely chop or chop by hand.
2. Place the parsnip 'rice' in a non-stick saucepan and add the can of evaporated milk and a can full of water. Stir in the honey, vanilla seeds and the pod.
3. Bring to the boil, reduce the heat and simmer over a medium heat for about 15 minutes, stirring occasionally, until rich and thick. Discard the vanilla pod.
4. Spoon into 4 small dishes and serve hot, or cool then chill before serving.

# YOGURT WHIP WITH TOFFEE APPLE AND RHUBARB

This is another lovely dessert where the whip is topped with yummy tangled toffee apple and rhubarb slices. You can use low-fat Greek yogurt and reduced-fat cream or cream substitute perfectly well in this recipe to reduce the saturated fat content. You must use thick outdoor rhubarb as the forced pink sticks are not tough enough to spiralize.

**Serves 4**

***For the yogurt whip***
**1 egg white**
**200g thick Greek-style plain yogurt**
**150ml double cream**
**1 tsp natural vanilla extract**
**1–2 tsp clear honey**

***For the toffee apple and rhubarb***
**2 eating apples, stalks removed**
**2 thick sticks of outdoor rhubarb**
**90g set honey**

1 Make the yogurt whip. Whip the egg white until peaking, then whisk the yogurt and cream together with the honey and vanilla until thick and peaking (I only use 1 tsp honey as I find the topping adds plenty of sweetness, but you may prefer a little more). Fold in the egg white with a metal spoon. Divide between 4 wine glasses or glass serving dishes. Chill in the fridge.

2 Spiralize the apples on the wide curls blade, stalk ends towards the blade. Discard any pips. Spiralize the rhubarb on the same blade. Dry thoroughly on kitchen paper.

3 Heat the honey in a non-stick saucepan until richly golden and caramelised. Add the apples and rhubarb. Quickly toss in the caramel so all are coated (be careful, they will bubble a lot). Allow to bubble until the juice evaporates and the apples and rhubarb are tender and bathed in caramel sauce. Leave to cool.

4 When ready to serve, top the yogurt whip with the toffee apples and rhubarb and serve.

# SPICED CARROT BUNS

Carrot cake is a long-term favourite; these little buns make a delicious change and it's so much easier to spiralize than to grate carrots! If you don't like nuts simply leave them out or add raisins instead.

**Makes 9**

**1 carrot, about 100g, peeled or scrubbed and halved widthways**
**50ml sunflower oil**
**1 egg**
**75g set honey**
**85g self-raising wholemeal flour (or plain wholemeal flour plus ¾ tsp baking powder)**
**¼ tsp bicarbonate of soda**
**½ tsp ground cinnamon**
**20g walnuts, chopped**

1. Spiralize the carrot on the 3mm noodle blade. Place in a food processor and pulse briefly to finely chop, or finely chop by hand.
2. Preheat the oven to 180°C/Gas 4. Line 9 sections of a tartlet tin with paper cake cases.
3. Whisk the oil, eggs and honey together until pale and thickened (I use a food mixer).
4. Mix the flour, bicarbonate of soda and cinnamon together. Sprinkle over the egg mixture, then fold in with a metal spoon. Fold in the carrots and walnuts.
5. Divide among the prepared cases. Bake for about 18 minutes or until risen, richly golden and the centres spring back when lightly pressed. Cool on a wire rack.

# SHREDDED PARSNIP AND GINGER CUPCAKES

These are lightly flavoured with ginger and topped with a rich soft cheese and honey frosting. Use the thin end of the parsnip to add to a soup or stock.

**Makes 12**

**1 parsnip, fat end only, about 120g, peeled and trimmed flat both ends**
**100g butter, softened**
**100g set honey**
**1 large egg**
**100g spelt flour**
**1½ tsp baking powder**
**1 tsp ground ginger**

***For the frosting***
**1 lemon**
**100g cream cheese**
**50g ground almonds**
**2 tbsp set honey**

1. Spiralize the parsnip on the 3mm noodle blade. Place in a food processor and roughly chop by pulsing a few times, or chop by hand.
2. Preheat the oven to 180°C/Gas 4. Line 12 sections of a tartlet tin with paper cake cases.
3. Beat the softened butter and honey together until light and fluffy. Beat in the egg to form a batter.
4. Sift the flour, baking powder and ginger over the top, add the parsnips and fold it all in with a metal spoon.
5. Divide the mixture among the paper cases and bake in the oven for about 18 minutes until risen, golden and the centres spring back when lightly pressed. Leave to cool on a wire rack.
6. Meanwhile, finely grate the zest of half the lemon into a bowl. Add the cream cheese, almonds and honey and beat together until fluffy. Chill until ready to use. When the cakes are cold, swirl the frosting on top. Coarsely grate the remaining lemon zest and pop a couple of pieces on top of each cake to decorate.

# APPLE CLUSTER CAKE

Spiralizing the apples is much quicker than coring and slicing them and you get a delicious-looking cluster effect on top. It's a cake that can be served warm for pudding with custard or cream or cold with a cup of coffee or tea.

**Makes 12 pieces**

**3 large Bramley cooking apples, about 750g, peeled**
**2 tbsp lemon juice**
**12 tbsp clear honey**
**2 eggs**
**85g butter, diced, plus extra for greasing**
**4 tbsp crème fraîche**
**3 tbsp apple juice**
**150g wholemeal flour, plus extra for dusting**
**2 tsp baking powder**
**½ tsp ground cinnamon**

1. Spiralize the apples on the wide curls blade, stalk ends towards the blade. Discard any pips. Toss the apple in the lemon juice to prevent browning, then add 3 tbsp of the honey and toss well to coat.
2. Preheat the oven to 190°C/Gas 5. Butter a 1.5 litre rectangular baking dish. Dust with a little wholemeal flour.
3. Whisk the eggs with 6 tbsp of the remaining honey until thick.

4 Heat the butter, crème fraîche and apple juice together until the butter melts. Bring to the boil, then pour onto the egg mixture and stir well.
5 Mix together the flour and baking powder. Sprinkle over the surface of the creamy mixture. Drain any juice that's collected with the apples over the flour and fold it all together with a metal spoon. Turn into the prepared dish.
6 Cover the surface with the tangled apples, Dust with the cinnamon. Bake in the oven for about 40 minutes or until cooked through and browned on top. Leave to cool for at least 10 minutes in the dish, then warm the remaining honey and brush over the top. Serve warm or leave until completely cold before cutting into pieces.

# SWEET POTATO BREAD

This is a delicious bread to slice and have toasted for breakfast, or equally delicious when fresh, served with cheese and pickles or as an accompaniment to any savoury recipe in this book. I use half wholemeal and half white flour for a lighter texture but still with plenty of fibre.

**Makes a 900g loaf**

**1 small sweet potato, about 175g, peeled and trimmed flat both ends**
**250g strong wholemeal flour**
**250g strong plain white flour**
**¾ tsp salt**
**2 tsp easy-blend dried yeast**
**1 tbsp olive oil**
**300ml hand-warm water**
**beaten egg or a little plain yogurt to glaze**

1. Spiralize the sweet potato on the 3mm noodle blade. Either place in a food processor and pulse a few times to finely chop, or finely chop by hand.
2. Mix the flours with the salt and yeast in a bowl or food processor. Add the oil, sweet potato and water and mix to form a soft but not too sticky dough. Either turn out of the bowl and knead on a lightly floured surface for about 5 minutes until elastic or, if you are using a processor, run the machine for 1–2 minutes to knead.

3 Cover the bowl with a clean cloth and leave in a warm place to rise for about an hour until almost doubled in bulk.

4 Oil a 900g loaf tin (or use a silicone one, in which case there is no need to grease). Knock back and re-knead the dough, then shape it into an oblong and place in the tin. Leave to rise again until the dough reaches the top of the tin – this may take a good hour. Meanwhile, preheat the oven to 220°C/Gas 7.

5 Gently brush the top of the loaf with beaten egg or yogurt. Bake in the oven for 50 minutes or until risen, deep golden and crusty (but cover loosely with foil after 30 minutes if over-browning). Tip out of the tin, return to the oven upside down and bake for a further 10 minutes or until the base is golden and sounds hollow when tapped with the knuckles.

6 Cool on a wire rack before slicing.

# SWEET POTATO KATAIFI

Kataifi is usually made with a finely shredded filo pastry dough. Here I've used strands of sweet potato to make the casing. These are not low-carb but I am not ashamed of that – they are a wonderful treat that's packed with good things and are delicious with some Greek yogurt for dessert or cut into small pieces to enjoy with a cup of coffee.

**Makes 9**

**2 small round sweet potatoes, about 400g total weight, peeled and trimmed flat both ends**
**4 tbsp wholemeal flour**
**75g butter, melted**

***For the filling***
**100g ground almonds**
**85g walnuts, finely chopped**
**60g stoned dates, finely chopped**
**1 tsp ground cinnamon**
**¼ tsp ground cloves**
**2 eggs, beaten**

***For the syrup***
**5 tbsp clear honey**
**1 tbsp water**
**1 tbsp lemon juice**

1. Spiralize the sweet potatoes on the 3mm noodle blade. Place in a bowl and add the wholemeal flour and 2 tbsp of the melted butter. Mix well.
2. To make the filling, stir all the ingredients except the eggs together, then blend in the eggs to form a lumpy paste.
3. Butter an 18cm square shallow baking tin with a little of the remaining butter and line it with non-stick baking paper.
4. Preheat the oven to 180°C/Gas 4 and place a baking sheet in the oven to heat. Press half the sweet potato mixture into the tin, pressing it well into the corners. Spread the filling mixture on top and spread out evenly, pressing down firmly with the fingers.
5. Top with the remaining sweet potatoes, spreading them out in an even, tangled layer, then brush with the remaining melted butter. Bake in the oven for 50 minutes until golden and cooked through.
6. About 5 minutes before the kataifi are ready, mix the syrup ingredients together in a small pan, bring to the boil and boil for 1 minute. Remove the kataifi from the oven and pour over the syrup to cover completely. Allow to soak in and for the mixture to cool completely. Cut into 9 pieces (or smaller, if preferred) and serve cold.

# INDEX